LOMA's

GLOSSARY

of Insurance
and Financial
Services
Terms

Edited by

Jane Lightcap Brown, Ph.D., FLMI, ALHC, ACS

2300 Windy Ridge Parkway, Suite 600
Atlanta, Georgia 30339-8443

PROJECT TEAM:

Project Editor	Jane Lightcap Brown, Ph.D., FLMI, ALHC, ACS
Manuscript Editor	Jo Ann Appleton, FLMI, ALHC
Project Manager	Joyce R. Abrams, J.D., FLMI, ACS, AIRC, AIAA, ALHC, PAHM, HIA, MHP
Production Manager	Michelle Stone Weathers, ACS
Print Buyer	Audrey H. Gregory
Production/Print Coordinator	Amy Souwan
Administrative Support	Aurelia Kennedy-Hemphill
Typography	Mary Rusch
Interior Design	Michelle Stone Weathers, ACS
Cover Design	Kathleen Ryan, FLMI, PCS, ARA, AIRC, AIAA, PAHM

Library of Congress Cataloging-in-Publication Data

LOMA's glossary of insurance and financial services terms / edited by Jo Ann Appleton, Jane Lightcap Brown.

    p. cm.
    ISBN 1-57974-152-5 (softcover)
    1. Insurance, Life--Dictionaries. 2. Insurance, Health--Dictionaries. 3. Employee fringe benefits--Dictionaries. 4. Financial services industry--Dictionaries. I. Title: Glossary of insurance and financial services terms. II. Appleton, Jo Ann S. III. Brown, Jane Lightcap.

HG8758 .L64 2002
368.3'003--dc21

                                    2002066061

ISBN 1-57974-152-5
Printed in the United States of America

About
LOMA's Glossary of Insurance and Financial Services Terms

Newly revised and expanded, *LOMA's Glossary of Insurance and Financial Services Terms* clarifies the specialized meanings of the terminology used in life and health insurance and financial services. Both industry novices and industry experts will find this glossary an essential tool in understanding industry principles and in communicating accurately with professionals in the financial services industry.

People who work in one area of an insurance or financial services organization usually learn the terminology used in their own area, but may be unfamiliar with the terms commonly used in other areas of their own companies and in other segments of the industry. To enhance understanding of the entire panorama of financial services activities, *LOMA's Glossary* spans every company area and presents clear, concise definitions, many with specific examples.

The insurance and financial services industry also uses dozens of acronyms, many apparently similar to one another. This glossary quickly directs readers to the full definitions of the terms referred to by such potentially confusing acronyms as DAC, DCAT, DFA, DPAC, DPSP, DRGs, and DST, to name only a few.

In addition, *LOMA's Glossary* distinguishes among and carefully defines the primary functions of dozens of industry organizations. The numerous cross-references help readers to locate information easily and to understand the often complex links among industry concepts.

As an industry leader, LOMA continually gathers new industry terminology and revises existing definitions as the industry changes. We welcome your suggestions to help make *LOMA's Glossary* an even more comprehensive and useful reference. Please send your suggestions and comments to

LOMA
Education & Training Division
2300 Windy Ridge Parkway, Suite 600
Atlanta, GA 30339-8443
Attn: LOMA's Glossary

You can also send an e-mail to education@loma.org.

Acknowledgements

We would like to thank the many industry experts who have provided invaluable help with this and previous editions of LOMA glossaries. By reviewing LOMA's insurance and financial services textbooks during development and by sharing information and industry knowledge, these professionals have offered excellent suggestions for improving the clarity and accuracy of glossary definitions and for including additional terms for the book. Their efforts have helped us to make this revision of *LOMA's Glossary* reflect the widespread and continuing evolution of the insurance and financial services industry.

We would also like to thank Susan Conant, FLMI, CEBS, HIA, PAHM, Senior Associate in LOMA's Education & Training Division, for reviewing the financial services terminology in this edition.

LOMA's
Glossary of Insurance
and Financial Services Terms

1035 exchange. *See* **Section 1035 Exchange.**

1099. *See* **IRS Form 1099.**

20 percent rule. *See* **percentage-of-income rule.**

401(k) plan. In the United States, a special type of profit-sharing plan, savings plan, or retirement plan that is established by employers for the benefit of employees and that allows both employers and employees to make specified contributions to the plan on a tax-deferred basis.

403(b) plan. In the United States, an arrangement that allows not-for-profit employers and their employees to make contributions to a tax-deferred retirement savings plan established for the benefit of employees.

457 plan. In the United States, an arrangement that allows state and local governments and their employees to make contributions to a tax-deferred retirement savings plan established for the benefit of employees.

5498. *See* **IRS Form 5498.**

AADLs. *See* **advanced activities of daily living.**

ABC. *See* **activity-based costing.**

absolute assignment. An irrevocable transfer of complete ownership of a life insurance policy or an annuity from one party to another. *Contrast with* **collateral assignment.** *See also* **assignment.**

ACB. *See* **adjusted cost basis.**

Accelerated Benefits Model Regulation. In the United States, a National Association of Insurance Commissioners (NAIC) model regulation designed to regulate accelerated death benefit provisions and to impose disclosure standards on insurers that provide such benefits.

accelerated death benefit. A benefit included in a life insurance policy or added to a life insurance policy through a policy rider that gives the policyowner the right to receive a portion—usually between 50 and 80 percent—of the policy's death benefit during the insured's lifetime when the insured is terminally ill as defined in the policy. Also known as *terminal illness (TI) benefit.*

acceptable alternative mechanism. For purposes of the Health Insurance Portability and Accountability Act (HIPAA) in the United States, a state-approved plan that provides health insurance coverage to all eligible individuals without imposing preexisting conditions exclusions and gives eligible individuals a choice of health insurance coverage.

accident insurance. A type of health insurance coverage that only provides benefits for an insured's death, dismemberment, disability, or medical care that results from the insured being in an accident. *See also* **health insurance.**

accidental death and dismemberment (AD&D) benefit. A supplementary life insurance policy benefit that provides for an amount of money in addition to the policy's basic death benefit. This additional amount is payable if the insured dies as the result of an accident or if the insured loses any two limbs or the sight in both eyes as the result of an accident.

accidental death benefit (ADB). A supplementary life insurance policy benefit that provides a death benefit in addition to the policy's basic death benefit if the insured's death occurs as the result of an accident. *See also* **double indemnity benefit.**

account. The basic tool that a company uses to record, group, and summarize similar types of financial transactions.

account fee. In unbundled variable insurance products, an annual charge to customers generally expressed as the lesser of a specified dollar amount or a percentage, such as 2 percent of the account value.

account form. The presentation format of a balance sheet in which asset accounts appear on the left side and liabilities and owners' equity accounts appear on the right side.

account payable. A liability account that represents a contractual promise of payment by the holder of the account to another party.

account receivable. An asset account that represents a contractual promise by another party to pay an amount to the holder of the account.

accounting. A system or set of rules and methods for collecting, recording, summarizing, reporting, and analyzing a company's financial information

accounting controls. The policies and procedures used to authorize financial transactions, safeguard assets, and provide reliable, timely, and fairly presented financial information about a company.

accounting entry. A record of a financial transaction that includes at least one debit and one credit and shows the monetary value of the transaction in balance on a specified date. *See also* **credit** and **debit.**

accredited reinsurer. A reinsurance company that is not licensed in the ceding company's jurisdiction, but meets specified financial and reporting requirements of that jurisdiction and holds a license in and is domiciled in at least one other jurisdiction.

accrual-basis accounting. An accounting system in which a company records revenues when they are earned and expenses when they are incurred, even if the company has not yet received the revenues or paid the expenses.

accrued income. (1) In accounting, income that has already been earned, but which is not receivable until a specified date in the next accounting period. (2) In investments, the amount of interest that has been earned on a bond, but which is not yet payable to the bondholder as of the financial reporting date.

accumulated cost of insurance. For a life insurance product at a specified point in time, the total amount the insurer has paid in benefits, accumulated at interest.

accumulated value. The total of an amount of money invested plus the interest earned by that money.

accumulated value of an annuity. At any given date during the accumulation period of a fixed deferred annuity, the net amount paid for the annuity, plus interest earned, less the amount of any withdrawals or surrender charges. The accumulated value of a variable, deferred annuity is calculated based on the value of the contract owner's interest in the separate accounts used to fund the annuity. Also known as *accumulation value of an annuity* and *account value of an annuity.*

accumulated value of net premiums. For a life insurance product at a specified point in time, the total of the net premiums collected, accumulated at interest.

accumulation at interest dividend option. An option, available to the owners of participating insurance policies, that allows a policyowner to leave policy dividends on deposit with the insurer and earn interest. *See also* **dividends** and **policy dividend options.**

accumulation period. For a deferred annuity contract, the time period between the date that the contract owner purchases the annuity and either (1) the date that periodic income payments begin or (2) the date that the contract's surrender value is paid. During the accumulation period, the accumulation value of the annuity account grows.

accumulation unit. A unit of measurement that represents an ownership share in a selected subaccount of a variable deferred annuity during its accumulation period. After the accumulation period ends, the accumulation units are used to buy annuity units. *See also* **accumulation period** and **annuity units.**

ACLF. *See* **adult congregate living facility.**

ACLI. *See* **American Council of Life Insurers.**

acquisition-cost concept. *See* **cost concept.**

acquisition expenses. Costs that are directly attributable to the production of new business. *See also* **policy acquisition expenses.**

actively-at-work provision. A group insurance policy provision which states that, in order to be eligible for coverage, an employee must be actively at work—rather than ill or on leave—on the day the coverage is to take effect. If the employee is not actively at work on that day, the group insurance coverage does not become effective until the next day that the employee is actively at work.

active management strategy. An investment strategy in which an asset manager views any security in a portfolio as potentially tradable, if doing so would improve the portfolio's performance. *See also* **portfolio** and **security.**

activities of daily living (ADLs). In long-term care insurance, activities such as eating, bathing, and dressing that an insured must be *unable* to perform in order to demonstrate a need for long-term care and, thus, qualify for long-term care benefits.

activity-based costing (ABC). An accounting method for estimating the price of a product or service that links costs to products based on the activities consumed in producing the products or services. *See also* **activity cost.**

activity cost. In activity-based costing (ABC), the cost attributable to a specified activity, such as telephone charges in an insurer's customer call center. *See also* **activity-based costing (ABC).**

activity ratios. Financial ratios, measuring the speed with which various assets are converted into sales or cash, that gauge the productivity and efficiency of a company. Also known as *operating efficiency ratios.*

actual cash value insurance. A type of homeowner's insurance that pays the policyholder an amount equal to the replacement cost of the property minus an amount for depreciation.

actual net debt. For purposes of determining the benefit payable under a consumer credit insurance policy, the lump-sum amount needed on any given date to pay off the debt, excluding un-earned interest and any other unearned finance charges.

actuarial assumptions. The estimated values—for such elements of insurance product design as mortality rates, investment earnings, expenses, and policy lapses—on which an insurer bases its product pricing and policy reserve calculations.

actuarial cost method. A formal approach used for preparing valuations of defined benefit pension plan liabilities in order to ensure that the plan is adequately and systematically funded. Also known as *actuarial funding method* and *pension plan valuation method.*

actuarial function. The area of an insurance company responsible for seeing that the company's operations are conducted on a mathematically sound basis. In conjunction with other depart-ments, it designs and revises a company's insurance products, establishes premium and dividend rates, determines what a company's reserve liabilities should be, and establishes nonforfei-ture, surrender, and loan values. It also does the research needed to predict mortality and morbidity rates, to establish guidelines for selecting risks, and to determine the profitability of the company's products.

actuarial funding method. *See* **actuarial cost method.**

actuarial liabilities. *See* **reserves.**

actuarial memorandum. A report, required in many U.S. policy form filings, which demonstrates that the policy in question complies with all state insurance laws and regulations that apply to the actuarial (mathematical) soundness of the policy.

Actuarial Opinion and Memorandum Regulation (AOMR). Under the Standard Valuation Law in the United States, a requirement for insurers to (1) submit an actuarial opinion to state in essence that the insurer's reserves and associated assets make adequate provision for anticipated cash flows arising from the insurer's contractual obligations and (2) prepare an actuarial memorandum in support of the opinion. This memorandum is not submitted unless requested by an insurance department.

actuarial opinion statement. In the United States, a separate document that must be submitted along with the Annual Statement by insurance companies that issue interest-sensitive products; this document represents an independent analysis of an insurance company's financial data.

actuarial valuation of pension plan benefits. The outcome or process of finding the actuarial present value, as of a specified valuation date, of a defined benefit pension plan's future benefit payments.

actuarial valuation. A determination by an actuary, based on statistical probability, of the value of assets and/or liabilities.

actuary. A technical expert in insurance, annuities, and financial instruments who applies mathematical knowledge to industry and company statistics to calculate an insurance company's mortality rates, morbidity rates, lapse rates, premium rates, policy reserves, and other financial values. *See also* **product actuary**, **valuation actuary**, and **appointed actuary**.

ADA. *See* **Americans with Disabilities Act**.

ADB. *See* **accidental death benefit**.

AD&D. *See* **accidental death and dismemberment benefit**.

additional insured rider. *See* **second insured rider**.

additional term insurance option. An option available to owners of participating insurance policies under which the insurer uses a policy dividend as a net single premium to purchase one-year term insurance on the insured's life. Also known as *fifth dividend option*. *See also* **dividend** and **policy dividend options**.

ADEA. *See* **Age Discrimination in Employment Act**.

adjustable life insurance. A form of life insurance that allows policyowners to vary the type of coverage provided by their policies as their insurance needs change.

adjusted cost basis (ACB). A measure of the cost of a life insurance policy at a given time.

adjusted premium. An amount used in the calculation of cash values for life insurance; this amount is equal to the policy's valuation net annual premium plus an amount added to account for an insurer's expenses.

adjusting entry. An accounting entry that a company makes to record internal financial transactions or correct errors that occur in one or more accounting periods.

adjustment methods provision. In an annuity contract, a written statement describing the steps the insurer will take to correct any material misstatement of age or sex. *See also* **misstatement of age or sex provision.**

ADLs. *See* **activities of daily living.**

administrative fee. For annuities, a fee charged by insurers to cover costs such as issuing a fixed or variable annuity, making administrative changes to the annuity contract, and preparing the contract owner's statement. In the case of some fixed annuity contracts, fees are not charged separately but have been included in the premiums charged for the contract. In other cases, a stated, flat dollar amount is automatically deducted from the customer's annuity account value each year. For variable annuities, the fee may be expressed as a percentage of the assets in the investment subaccounts. Also known as *administration charge, administration expense fee,* and *contract fee.*

administrative services only (ASO) contract. A contract under which an insurer or other organization, such as a third-party administrator, agrees to provide administrative services for an employer that is self-funding an insurance benefit plan rather than purchasing group insurance. *See also* **third-party administrator (TPA).**

Administrative Supervision Model Act. In the United States, a National Association of Insurance Commissioners (NAIC) model law that authorizes the insurance commissioner of an insurer's state of domicile to place the insurer under administrative supervision. *See also* **administrative supervision.**

administrative supervision. A legal condition under which an insurer in the United States may be required to obtain the permission of the insurance commissioner of its domiciliary state before the insurer takes any of a variety of specified actions. *See also* **Administrative Supervision Model Act.**

admitted assets. For an insurer, assets whose full value can be reported on the Assets page of the U.S. Annual Statement. *Contrast with* **nonadmitted assets.**

admitted reinsurer. *See* **authorized reinsurer.**

adult congregate living facility (ACLF). In long-term care insurance, a type of assisted living facility designed mostly for middle- to lower-income groups, with less spacious living quarters than continuing care retirement communities and meals served in a central dining room.

adult day care. In long-term care insurance, care provided to adults in a group setting during hours when primary caregivers are working.

advance and arrears system. A premium accounting method used in the home service distribution system under which the home service company charges the individual agent with the amount of all premiums due on the policies the agent services. When the agent sends the collected premiums, the company credits the agent with the amount of premiums collected. *See also* **home service system** and **industrial insurance.**

advanced activities of daily living (AADLs). In long-term care insurance, vocational, social, or recreational activities that reflect personal choice and add meaning and richness to a person's life. The AADLs include working; attending church; going out to dinner, a theater, or a concert; playing cards; participating in physical recreational activities; and driving an automobile.

advanced underwriting department. A department within an insurance company that assists agents with estate planning and business insurance cases; this department prepares proposals based on the information the agent has collected; accompanies the agent, if requested, on sales presentations; provides computer support services; and conducts seminars and counsels agents regarding tax laws and methods of using insurance products to solve estate planning problems.

adverse action. According to the Fair Credit Reporting Act in the United States, (1) a denial or revocation of credit, a change in the terms of an existing credit arrangement, or a refusal to grant credit in substantially the amount or on substantially the terms requested; or (2) a denial or cancellation of insurance, an increase in any charge for insurance, a reduction in coverage, or any other adverse or unfavorable change in the terms or amount of existing insurance or coverage applied for by a consumer.

adverse deviation. In insurance product design, a difference between actual and assumed product values that produces a decrease in actual product profitability relative to assumed product profitability. *Contrast with* **favorable deviation**.

adverse selection. *See* **antiselection**.

adverse underwriting decision. An underwriting decision in which an insurer refuses to issue insurance coverage to an applicant, terminates existing coverage, or offers to provide an applicant with insurance at higher than standard premium rates.

advertisement. According to the National Association of Insurance Commissioners (NAIC) Rules Governing the Advertising of Life Insurance, any material designed (1) to create public interest in life insurance or annuities, an insurer, or an insurance producer or (2) to induce the public to purchase, increase, modify, reinstate, borrow on, surrender, replace, or retain a policy.

affiliate reinsurer. A type of captive reinsurer that is established for use by a group of affiliated insurers. *See also* **captive reinsurer**.

after-tax dollars. Money after taxes have been paid on it.

Age Discrimination in Employment Act (ADEA). A United States federal law that protects workers age 40 and older from being discriminated against because of their age.

age provision. An annuity contract provision that specifies a maximum issue age for annuitants, typically between 70 and 85 years old.

agency. A legal relationship in which one party, known as the *principal*, authorizes another party, known as the *agent*, to act on the principal's behalf. *See also* **agent** and **principal**.

agency administration. All of the activities performed by an insurer's home office employees or by field office personnel to provide support and service to the insurer's field force. *See also* **field force**.

agency agreement. A written contract that spells out the rights and duties of a principal and an agent and the scope of the agent's actual authority. Also known as *agency contract*. *See also* **agent** and **principal**.

agency-building distribution system. A type of insurance sales distribution system wherein companies recruit and train their salespeople, and provide them with financial support and office facilities. Four general types of agency-building distribution systems are ordinary agency distribution systems, multiple-line agency (MLA) systems, salaried sales distribution systems, and location-selling distribution systems. *Contrast with* **nonagency building distribution system.** *See also* **location-selling distribution systems, multiple-line agency (MLA) systems, ordinary agency distribution systems,** and **salaried sales distribution systems.**

agency contract. *See* **agency agreement.**

agency distribution plan. A document that describes an insurance company's goals and objectives for product distribution and serves as a guide for each field office's own operating plan.

agency system. *See* **agency-building distribution system.**

agent. (1) In agency law, a party who is authorized by another party, the *principal*, to act on the principal's behalf in contractual dealings with third parties. *See also* **principal.** (2) In insurance, any person or entity representing an insurance company and selling insurance. *See also* **agent-broker, broker, general agent (GA),** and **personal producing general agent (PPGA).**

agent-broker. A career insurance agent who places business with a primary company and with other insurance companies.

agents' debit balances. Amounts that sales agents have collected from customers and owe to an insurer.

agent's statement. A portion of the insurance application that contains the agent's comments about or impressions of the proposed insured and the risk involved; this statement is usually not made a part of the policy contract.

aggregate level cost allocation methods. Pension plan valuation methods that measure costs directly for an entire pension plan without attribution to individual plan participants. Also known as *aggregate level-premium cost methods. Contrast with* **individual level cost allocation methods.**

aggregate level-premium cost methods. *See* **aggregate level cost allocation methods.**

aggregate stop-loss coverage. A type of stop loss insurance coverage purchased by self-insured employers that provides benefits to the employer when total group health claims exceed a stated dollar amount within a stated period of time. *See also* **individual stop-loss coverage.**

aggregation rule. A United States federal income tax rule stating that all deferred annuity contracts that were entered into after October 21, 1988, and that were issued by the same insurer to the same contract owner during the same calendar year, will be treated as one contract for purposes of determining the amount of any withdrawal that is included in income.

aggressive financial strategy. A financial management strategy that places an unusually strong emphasis on profitability and de-emphasizes solvency.

AICPA. *See* **American Institute of Certified Public Accountants.**

AIR. *See* **assumed investment return.**

aleatory contract. A contract in which one party provides something of value to another party in exchange for a conditional promise, which is a promise that the other party will perform a stated act upon the occurrence of an uncertain event. Insurance contracts are aleatory because the policyowner pays premiums to the insurer, and in return the insurer promises to pay benefits if the event insured against occurs. *Contrast with* **commutative contract.**

alien corporation. From the point of view of any state in the United States, a company that is incorporated under the laws of another country. *Contrast with* **domestic corporation.**

allied medical practitioner. A licensed health care provider who is not a licensed medical doctor; for example, chiropractors, osteopaths, or nurse midwives.

allocated pension funding contract. A type of pension plan contract in which all of the plan sponsor's contributions are credited to individuals in a manner that gives the individual-participants a legally enforceable claim to the benefits attributable to those contributions. *Contrast with* **unallocated pension funding contract.**

allowable expenses. According to the coordination of benefits provision included in most group medical expense insurance policies, those reasonable and customary expenses that the insured incurred and that are covered under at least one of the insured's group medical expense plans.

allowance. In a reinsurance arrangement, the reinsurer's proportionate share of the agent commissions, underwriting costs, administration costs, policy issue costs, and other expenses that an insurer incurs in acquiring a policy.

all-risk policy. A type of homeowner's insurance that covers losses caused by all perils other than those excluded in the policy.

ALM. *See* **asset/liability management.**

alpha split. *See* **alphabetic split.**

alphabetic split. A method insurance companies use to transfer excess risk to two or more reinsurers by assigning cases to each reinsurer according to policyowners' last names. Also known as *alpha split. See also* **reinsurance.**

alternate care benefits. In long-term care insurance (LTC) plans, benefits for nonconventional services developed cooperatively by a physician and an insurer to substitute for more expensive nursing home care. May include special medical care and treatments, different sites of care, or even medically necessary modifications to an insured person's home.

amendment. A provision added to a contract that modifies an existing provision.

American Academy of Actuaries. A professional organization of actuaries in the United States.

American Council of Life Insurers (ACLI). A U.S. organization that collects and disseminates data on life insurance markets.

American Institute of Certified Public Accountants (AICPA). A professional association of U.S. Certified Public Accountants (CPAs) that directly influences accounting practice in the United States in a variety of ways, including the development of generally accepted auditing standards (GAAS).

Americans with Disabilities Act (ADA). A U.S. federal law that protects disabled individuals against all types of discrimination, including employment discrimination.

amortized cost. An asset's historical cost, less any adjustment, such as depreciation or amortization, to the asset's book value.

analytical phase of IRIS. The second phase of the Insurance Regulatory Information System (IRIS) used in the United States to monitor the financial condition of insurers. IRIS was established and is operated by the National Association of Insurance Commissioners (NAIC). During this phase, NAIC examiners apply qualitative and quantitative standards to further analyze the Annual Statement data of insurers that had a number of unusual ratios during the first phase of IRIS analysis. *See also* **Insurance Regulatory Information System (IRIS)** and **statistical phase of IRIS.**

annual annuity. An annuity that provides for a series of annual benefit payments.

annual percentage rate (APR). *See* **effective interest rate.**

annual policy report. A statement an insurer issues at the end of each policy year to a policyowner to provide a summary of policy transactions that year.

annual report. (1) A financial document that an incorporated business issues to its stockholders, and other interested parties, to report the business's activities and financial status for a specified period, which is usually the preceding year. (2) A report that an insurer must provide to variable insurance contract owners describing the investment performance of subaccounts for the preceding year.

annual reset method. A method for crediting excess interest to an equity-indexed annuity that involves comparing the value of the index at the start of the contract year with its value at the end of the contract year. The starting value for the next year is reset to the value of the index at the end of the current contract year. The insurer determines the amount of excess interest by averaging the results for each contract year of the contract term. Also known as *ratchet method.*

Annual Return. In Canada, an accounting report that presents information about an insurer's operations and financial performance which every company subject to federal regulation must file with the Office of the Superintendent of Financial Institutions.

Annual Statement. A financial report that every insurer in the United States must file at least annually with the National

Association of Insurance Commissioners (NAIC) and the insurance regulatory organization in each state in which the insurer conducts business. Regulators use the information in the report to evaluate an insurance company's solvency and its compliance with insurance laws.

annualized premium. In the home service insurance distribution system, the amount of premium scheduled to be paid to an insurer for all the insurance policies in an agent's book of business during the course of one year.

annually renewable term (ART) insurance. *See* **yearly renewable term (YRT) insurance.**

annuitant. The person whose lifetime is used to measure the length of time periodic income payments are payable under an annuity contract and who usually receives the annuity benefit payments.

annuitization period. *See* **payout period.**

annuitization. An annuity contract payout option that provides annuity benefit payments that are tied to the life expectancy of the annuitant.

annuity. (1) A series of periodic payments. (2) A financial contract between an insurer and a customer under which the insurer promises to make a series of periodic benefit payments to a named individual—the *payee*—in exchange for the contract owner's payment of a premium or series of premiums to the insurer. *See also* **annuity certain, annuity due, deferred annuity, ordinary annuity,** and **straight life annuity.**

annuity beneficiary. The person or party named to receive any survivor benefits that are payable during the accumulation period of a deferred annuity. *See also* **survivor benefits.**

annuity certain. A type of annuity contract that pays periodic income benefits for a stated period of time, regardless of whether the annuitant lives or dies. Also known as *period certain annuity. Contrast with* **straight life annuity.** *See also* **payout options.**

annuity contract. *See* **annuity.**

annuity conversion cost. The amount that a deferred annuity contract owner pays to obtain a specified dollar amount of periodic income payment upon annuitization of the contract. *Contrast with* **annuity purchase cost.**

annuity cost. A monetary amount that is equal to the present value of future periodic income payments under an annuity. *See also* **gross annuity cost, net annuity cost,** and **income date**.

annuity cost factor. A factor provided for use in determining the price or cost for a given amount of periodic income payment under an annuity payout option. An *annuity conversion factor* is the type of annuity cost factor used for converting a deferred annuity to an immediate annuity. An *annuity purchase factor* is the type of annuity cost factor used when a new customer purchases an immediate annuity.

annuity date. *See* **income date.**

Annuity Disclosure Model Regulation. In the United States, a National Association of Insurance Commissioners (NAIC) model regulation that requires insurers to provide prospective purchasers of specified types of annuities with information to help them select an annuity appropriate to their needs.

annuity due. A series of periodic payments for which the payment occurs at the beginning of each payment period. Also known as *annuity in advance. Contrast with* **ordinary annuity.**

annuity immediate. *See* **ordinary annuity.**

annuity in advance. *See* **annuity due.**

annuity in arrears. *See* **ordinary annuity.**

annuity mortality table. A chart that shows the projected mortality rates for persons purchasing annuities. Actuaries use annuity mortality tables to calculate premiums and reserves for annuities. Annuity mortality tables usually project lower rates of mortality than do mortality tables that are used for life insurance. *See also* **mortality rate** and **mortality table.**

annuity payee. *See* **payee.**

annuity period. The time span between each of the payments in a series of periodic annuity payments; for example, if benefits are payable monthly, then the annuity period is one month.

annuity purchase cost. Amount paid by the owner of an immediate annuity contract to obtain a specified dollar amount of periodic income payment upon annuitization of the contract. *Contrast with* **annuity conversion cost.**

annuity unit. A share in an insurer's variable subaccounts that determines the size of an annuitant's benefit payments during the payout period of a variable deferred annuity. *See* **accumulation unit, payout period,** and **subaccount.**

antiselection. The tendency of individuals who suspect or know they are more likely than average to experience loss to apply for or renew insurance to a greater extent than people who lack such knowledge of probable loss. Also known as *adverse selection* and *selection against the company.*

antitrust laws. In the United States, federal and state laws designed to protect commerce from unlawful restraints of trade, price discrimination, price fixing, and monopolies.

AOMR. *See* **Actuarial Opinion and Memorandum Regulation.**

APL provision. *See* **automatic premium loan provision.**

apparent authority. Authority that is not expressly given to an agent, but that a principal either intentionally or negligently allows a third party to believe the agent possesses.

applicant. In the insurance industry, the person or business that applies for an insurance policy or annuity contract.

appointed actuary. An actuary who has been duly appointed by an insurer's board of directors to render an official opinion as to the insurer's financial condition. *See also* **actuarial memorandum.**

appointment. A written statement from an officer of a licensed insurer that accompanies the application for an agent's license and that indicates that the insurer appoints the applicant as an agent to sell a particular line or lines of insurance for the insurer.

appropriated surplus. *See* **special surplus.**

APR. *See* **effective interest rate.**

APS. *See* **attending physician's statement.**

ART insurance. *See* **yearly renewable term insurance.**

articles. In reinsurance, the standard provisions found in many reinsurance treaties.

articles of incorporation. In the United States, the document that organizers of a company seeking incorporation must file with a state agency. The document contains the essential features of a proposed company, including its name, the location of its principal place of business, the kind of business it will transact, and the names of its original directors. *See also* **certificate of incorporation.**

ASA. *See* **Associate of the Society of Actuaries.**

ASO contract. *See* **administrative services only contract.**

assessment method. A historical method of funding life insurance in which the participants in an insurance plan prepaid an equal portion of the estimated annual cost of the plan's death benefits. If actual costs were less than expected, then participants received refunds. If costs were more than expected, then participants paid an additional amount. *See also* **mutual benefit method.**

asset allocation. The process of investing money in predetermined proportions in different types of assets to create a collection of assets with the desired expected return and the desired expected risk characteristics.

asset-based commissions. For annuities, commissions calculated on the basis of an annuity contract's accumulated value and growth, after an initial commission was paid upon the initial premium at the inception of the contract. Also known as *trail commissions*.

asset class. A group of similar investment instruments linked by related risk and return features.

asset fluctuation reserve. In the United States, a statutory reserve designed to absorb gains and losses in an insurer's investment portfolio. *See also* **asset valuation reserve** and **interest maintenance reserve.**

asset-liability management (ALM). A system that coordinates the administration of an insurer's obligations to customers with the administration of the insurer's investment portfolios so as to achieve the best possible financial effects.

asset management fee. A fee insurers charge for variable annuities to cover the costs of managing and operating the investment funds underlying the variable subaccounts. Asset management fees are generally a percentage of the dollar amount invested in each fund, with the percentage varying for each fund.

asset risk. *See* **C-1 risk.**

assets. The items of value owned by an individual or a company. Examples of assets include cash, computer equipment, investments, buildings, furniture, and land. *See also* **intangible assets** and **tangible assets.**

asset share. For an annuity or a life insurance product at a given time, the net amount of cash that the product has accumulated per unit of product. The applicable units of product differ for annuities and life insurance so that, for an annuity product at a given time, the asset share is the net amount of cash that the annuity product has accumulated per unit of annuity premium. For a life insurance product at a given time, the asset share is the net amount of cash that the product has accumulated per unit of face amount.

asset-share model. A mathematical simulation model that insurance companies use to illustrate how a product's assets, liabilities, and surplus would change from year to year under given sets of conditions. *See* **asset share**.

asset valuation reserve (AVR). A reserve account that insurers in the United States use to absorb changes in the value of assets caused by credit-related factors. Capital gains increase the AVR, while capital losses decrease the AVR.

assigned surplus. *See* **special surplus**.

assignee. A person or party to whom a property owner transfers some or all of the property owner's rights in a particular property by means of an assignment. *See also* **assignment** and **assignor**.

assignment. An agreement under which one party—the *assignor*—transfers some or all of his ownership rights in a particular property, such as a life insurance policy or an annuity contract, to another party—the *assignee*. *See also* **absolute assignment** and **collateral assignment**.

assignment of benefits. A statement on a medical expense claim form that, if signed by the claimant, directs an insurer to pay benefits directly to a health care provider rather than to the claimant.

assignment provision. An individual life insurance and annuity policy provision that describes the roles of the insurer and the policyowner when the policy is assigned.

assignor. A property owner who transfers some or all of the ownership rights in a particular property to another party by means of an assignment. *See also* **assignment** and **assignee**.

assisted living facility. In long-term care (LTC) insurance, a residential facility designed to meet (LTC) needs by providing accommodations and access to medical services.

Associate of the Society of Actuaries (ASA). A professional designation that an actuary may use upon completion of a specified series of examinations administered by the Society of Actuaries.

association examination. A method for examining the operations of multi-state insurance companies that was developed by the states and is recommended by the National Association of Insurance Commissioners (NAIC). According to this system, each insurer is domiciled within one of four geographic zones and examiners representing various states in a zone are responsible for conducting examinations of insurers within that zone. *See also* **financial condition examination, market conduct examination**, and **on-site regulatory examination**.

association group. A type of group that generally is eligible for group insurance and that consists of members of an association of individuals formed for a purpose other than to obtain insurance coverage, such as teachers' associations and physicians' associations.

assumed investment return (AIR). For variable annuity contracts, the total return that the subaccount investments must earn in order for annuity payments to remain the same from period to period under a variable payout option.

assuming company. *See* **reinsurer**.

assumption. In reinsurance, an insurer's act of accepting an insurance risk from another insurer.

assumption certificate. An insurance certificate issued to an insurer's existing policyowners to show that a reinsurer has assumed from the issuing company all of the risk under the policies. *See also* **assumption reinsurance**.

assumption reinsurance. A type of reinsurance that involves the total and permanent transfer of risk from the issuing company to a reinsurer. In assumption reinsurance, a reinsurer purchases a block of in-force insurance, creating contractual relationships with all insureds and assuming responsibility for policy administration and all liabilities. *Contrast with* **indemnity** and **reinsurance**. *See also* **reinsurance**.

Assumption Reinsurance Model Act. In the United States, a National Association of Insurance Commissioners (NAIC) model law designed to regulate insurers that assume or transfer risks under an assumption reinsurance agreement.

attachment point. In nonproportional reinsurance, an amount over which a reinsurer agrees to start paying benefits. *See also* **nonproportional reinsurance.**

attained age. For insurance purposes, the current age of an insured.

attained age conversion. The conversion of a term life insurance policy to a permanent plan of insurance at a premium rate that is based on the insured's age when the coverage is converted. *Contrast with* **original age conversion.** *See also* **conversion provision.**

attending physician. For underwriting purposes, a physician who has given or is giving medical care to a proposed insured. *Contrast with* **examining physician.**

attending physician's statement (APS). A written statement from a physician who has treated, or is currently treating, a proposed insured or an insured for one or more conditions. The statement provides the insurance company with information relevant to underwriting a risk or settling a claim.

audit. The process of examining and evaluating a company's records and procedures to ensure that accounting records and financial statements are accurate and reliable, the company maintains quality assurance, and operational procedures and policies are effective and legally compliant.

auditor's opinion. A statement, prepared by an independent public accounting company, that attests that the information contained in a company's annual report fairly represents the operations of the company and that the audit was conducted in accordance with generally accepted auditing standards (GAAS).

audit trail. A chronological, sequential set of accounting records and reports from the beginning to the end of a business transaction.

authorization to release information. A section of a claimant's statement that permits an insurer to obtain claim-specific information from medical caregivers and institutions, government agencies, other insurers, consumer reporting agencies, and other sources.

authorized reinsurer. A reinsurance company that is licensed or otherwise recognized by the insurance department in the jurisdiction of a ceding company. Also known as *admitted reinsurer. See also* **reinsurer.**

automatic binding limit. Under an automatic reinsurance agreement, the maximum dollar amount of risk the reinsurer will accept on a life without making its own underwriting assessment of the risk.

automatic dividend option. For participating life insurance policies, a specified policy dividend option that an insurance company will apply if the policyowner does not choose an option. The specified option typically is the paid-up additional insurance option.

automatic dollar cost averaging. A process whereby a variable annuity contract owner deposits premiums directly into a fixed account or money market account, and the insurer transfers a portion of this money on a regular basis into one or more of the insurer's variable subaccounts.

automatic nonforfeiture benefit. The specified nonforfeiture benefit that becomes effective automatically when a renewal premium for a permanent life insurance policy is not paid by the end of the grace period and the insured has not elected another nonforfeiture option. The most typical automatic nonforfeiture option is the extended term insurance benefit.

automatic premium loan (APL) provision. A permanent life insurance policy nonforfeiture provision that allows an insurer to automatically pay an overdue premium for a policyowner by making a loan against the policy's cash value as long as the cash value equals or exceeds the amount of the premium due. *See also* **nonforfeiture options.**

automatic rebalancing provision. A variable annuity contract provision which states that values automatically will be transferred between specified accounts to maintain the asset allocation percentages designated by the contract owner.

automatic reinsurance. A type of reinsurance under which a reinsurer agrees to automatically accept, within limits, the risks transferred by a ceding company. In this agreement, the ceding company assumes full underwriting responsibility for all cases reinsured. *Contrast with* **facultative reinsurance.** *See also* **reinsurance.**

automobile insurance. A type of insurance that protects an insured from financial losses arising from the operation of a vehicle.

AVR. *See* **asset valuation reserve.**

backdating. A practice by which an insurer makes the effective date of a life insurance policy earlier than the date of the application for the policy so that the premium rate will be lower. Also known as *dating back.*

back-end load. A surrender charge. For mutual funds or variable annuities, a sales charge that the share owner or contract owner pays upon withdrawing funds from the arrangement. Also known as *contingent deferred sales charge. Contrast with* **front-end load** and **no-load fund.**

back-loaded policy. A life insurance policy or a deferred annuity contract in which most of the expense charges occur when the policy owner or contract owner surrenders the policy or makes cash withdrawals from the policy. *Contrast with* **front-loaded policy.**

bailout provision. An annuity contract provision that enables the contract owner to surrender the annuity contract, usually without a surrender charge, if renewal interest rates on a fixed annuity fall below a pre-established level, typically 1 percent below the initial interest rate. Also known as *escape clause* and *cash-out provision.*

balance sheet. A financial statement that shows a company's financial condition or position as of a specified date; summarizes what a company owns (assets), what it owes (liabilities), and its owners' investment in the company (owners' equity) on a specified date. Also known as *statement of financial position.*

balance sheet equation. *See* **basic accounting equation.**

balanced mutual fund. A mutual fund that has the objective of preservation of capital with moderate income and growth in value.

bancassurance company. *See* **bank insurance company.**

bank insurance. Insurance coverage that is manufactured and underwritten by a commercial bank's own insurance company and distributed through the bank's distribution channels.

bank insurance company. A company that offers both banking and insurance services. Also known as *bancassurance company*.

bank line. *See* line of credit

bank reconciliation. The process of identifying and explaining the difference between the balance presented on a bank statement and the balance in the accounting records of an individual or a company. Insurers sometimes refer to this process as the *book balance*.

bank-sold insurance. A type of location-selling insurance distribution system in which insurance is distributed by a bank and manufactured and underwritten by an insurance company.

base period. The earliest financial reporting period used in horizontal analysis. *See also* **horizontal analysis**.

basic accounting equation. The formula that expresses the relationship among the three key account classifications—assets, liabilities, and owners' equity—on the balance sheet. Also known as *balance sheet equation*.

basic health care services. According to the National Association of Insurance Commissioners (NAIC) Health Maintenance Organizations (HMO) Model Act, specified medically necessary services that HMOs must provide to enrollees, such as preventive care, emergency care, inpatient and outpatient hospital care, diagnostic laboratory services, and diagnostic and therapeutic radiological services.

basic illustration. A spreadsheet, a ledger, or a proposal used in the sale of life insurance that falls under the scope of the National Association of Insurance Commissioners (NAIC) Life Insurance Illustrations Model Regulation and that shows both guaranteed and nonguaranteed elements of the policy. *See also* **illustration**.

basic mortality table. A mortality table that has no safety margin built into the mortality rates and that is used for the technical design of life insurance and annuity products. *Contrast with* **select mortality table** and **ultimate mortality table**.

basis point (bp). An increment of one-hundredth of a percent (0.01 percent); e.g., half a percent is equal to 50 bp, and one and a half percent is equal to 150 bp. Insurers often use this unit of measurement in calculating interest margins for insurance products with a significant investment component. *See also* **interest margin**.

bed reservation benefit. A long-term care (LTC) policy benefit that pays an amount to reserve a bed in a nursing home or other LTC facility while the insured person is hospitalized for treatment.

before-tax dollars. Money that has not been taxed.

benchmarking. The process by which a company compares its own performance, products, and services with those of other organizations that are recognized as the best in a particular category. The product or service that is determined to be the industry standard is known as a *benchmark*.

beneficiary. The person or legal entity the owner of an insurance policy names to receive the policy benefit if the event insured against occurs. *See also* **annuity beneficiary, contingent beneficiary**, and **irrevocable beneficiary**.

beneficiary for value. According to laws that are no longer in force in the common law jurisdictions of Canada, a life insurance policy beneficiary who has vested rights to policy proceeds because the beneficiary provided the policyowner with valuable consideration. Although the law no longer exists, some of these beneficiary designations continue to remain in effect in older policies.

benefit. (1) For an insurance contract, the amount of money that is paid as compensation when the loss insured against occurs. (2) For an annuity contract, the periodic payments made as specified in the contract.

benefit expenses. For insurers, the cost of paying contractual obligations to customers. Also known as *expense for contractual benefits* and *benefit costs. Contrast with* **operating expenses**.

benefit formula. For pension plans, a statement that describes a pension plan sponsor's financial obligation to plan participants.

benefit period. The specified time during which benefits will be paid under certain types of health insurance coverages. (1) For disability income coverage, the length of time during which disability income benefits are paid, typically lasting from less than a year to age 65 or 70. (2) For long-term care coverage, the number of days, months, or years during which a LTC policy will pay a daily benefit amount.

benefits budget. A type of budget indicating the amount of money an insurer expects to pay for claims, cash surrenders, and policy dividends during the next accounting period.

benefit schedule. *See* **schedule of benefits.**

benefits survey. A report that contains information on the benefits being offered to employees in a specified geographic area or industry.

benefit transmittal. A document compiled by a prospective group insurance policyholder for a group insurer that provides details concerning the insurance benefits being requested for each employee class, the effective date of coverage, how premium billing and claims will be administered, and other information concerning the type of plan being requested.

benefit unit. *See* **unit of coverage.**

bilateral contract. A contract between two parties who both make legally enforceable promises when they enter into the contract. *Contrast with* **unilateral contract.**

binding limit. *See* **automatic binding limit.**

binding premium receipt. *See* **temporary insurance agreement.**

blended rating. A process for calculating premium rates for group insurance that combines manual rating and experience rating; underwriters assign a credibility factor to the group's experience and include that factor in the premium calculations. *See also* **experience rating** and **manual rating.**

block of business. In insurance, a large number of similar life insurance policies or annuity contracts.

block of policies. A group of policies issued to insureds who are all the same age, the same sex, and in the same risk classification.

blood chemistry profile. A laboratory test that identifies various aspects of possible chronic and acute diseases in a sample of blood. Underwriters commonly order this laboratory test as part of the risk selection process for life insurance and health insurance.

bond. A debt security whereby the bond issuer promises to pay the bondholder a stated rate of interest over a specified period of time, at the end of which time, the original amount of borrowed money must be repaid. The owner of the bond is known as the *bondholder.* The entity that sells the bond to raise money is known as the *bond issuer.*

bond principal. The sum the issuer of a bond borrows from the bond's initial purchaser. This amount which is stated on the face of the bond is payable by the issuer of the bond on or before the bond's maturity date. Also known as bond's *face value*, *maturity value*, and *par value*.

bond rating. A letter grade assigned by a bond rating agency that indicates the credit quality of a bond issue.

bond subaccount. One of the three main asset classes in an insurance company's separate account within which owners of variable insurance contracts can deposit funds and have the funds invested in a variety of both short-term and long-term government and corporate bonds. *See also* **money market subaccount** and **stock subaccount**.

bonus additions. In Canada, additional amounts of paid-up life insurance or one-year term life insurance acquired through a life insurance policyowner's dividend payout option.

book balance. *See* **bank reconciliation**.

book value. The value at which an asset is recorded in a company's accounting records.

bordereau. In reinsurance, a regular report that is exchanged between a ceding company and a reinsurer.

bottom-up budgeting. A budget-setting approach for business organizations that requires lower-level managers to prepare their own departmental budgets for approval by upper-level managers.

boycott. An agreement among competing companies to refrain from doing business with another company.

bp. *See* **basis point**.

branch manager. In the insurance industry, the person who heads a field office of an insurance company that uses the branch office distribution system. This individual recruits, selects, and trains career agents, and acts as the sales manager for the geographic area covered by the sales office. Also known as *general manager*.

branch office distribution system. A type of ordinary agency insurance distribution system wherein companies establish and maintain field offices in key areas throughout a marketing territory that are headed by a branch manager. *See also* **branch manager** and **ordinary agency distribution system**.

breakeven analysis. *See* **cost-volume-profit (CVP) analysis.**

break-even period. *See* **validation period.**

break even point. The point at which a product's revenues are equal to its costs. *See also* **validation point.**

broker. (1) Any person or entity engaged in the business of buying or selling investment securities for the account of another. *Contrast with* **dealer.** (2) An insurance sales agent who sells insurance products for more than one insurance company. *Contrast with* **captive agent.**

brokerage distribution system. A type of nonagency building insurance distribution system that relies on the use of agent-brokers and brokers to sell and deliver insurance and annuity products. *See also* **agent-broker, broker,** and **nonagency building distribution system.**

broker-dealer. A person or firm that provides information or advice to customers regarding the sale and/or purchase of securities, serves as a financial intermediary between buyers and sellers of securities, and supervises the sales process to make sure that salespeople comply with all applicable regulations.

budget. A financial plan of action, expressed in monetary terms, which covers a specified time period, such as one year.

build chart. A chart that underwriters use to assess the degree of risk a proposed insured represents. The chart indicates average weights for various heights for each sex, along with the mortality debits associated with increases in weight.

bulk administration. A method of reinsurance administration in which the ceding company administers the reinsurance and periodically submits summarized reports on premiums and on the policies to the reinsurer, but does not provide individualized detailed information about risks reinsured until a claim needs to be processed.

bundled product structure. Insurance or annuity product design in which an insurer presents the product to customers as a package of benefits, provided in exchange for a given payment. The mortality, investment, and expense factors are not identified separately in the product. *Contrast with* **unbundled product structure.**

business continuation insurance plan. An insurance plan designed to enable a business owner (or owners) to provide for the business' continued operation if the owner or a key person dies. *See also* **partnership insurance.**

business financial supplement. A specialized questionnaire used in underwriting business insurance that requests information about the type of business, the current financial condition of the business, and the purpose for which the insurance is being requested.

business overhead expense coverage. Disability coverage that provides benefits designed to pay a disabled insured's share of a business' overhead expenses.

Buyer's Guide. A publication designed to educate consumers about life insurance or annuity products and enable them to get the most for their money when shopping for these products. In the United States, many states have enacted legislation that requires insurers to provide prospective buyers of certain insurance and annuity products with a Buyer's Guide. *See also* **Guide to Buying Life Insurance.**

buy-sell agreement. An agreement in which one party agrees to purchase the financial interest that a second party has in a business following the second party's death, and (2) the second party agrees to direct his estate to sell his interest in the business to the purchasing party.

C risks (contingency risks). In the United States, four officially recognized categories of risk that the actuarial profession has identified as being vital to insurers. *See also* **C-1 risk (asset risk), C-2 risk (pricing risk), C-3 risk (interest-rate risk),** and **C-4 risk (general management risk).**

C-1 risk (asset risk). For insurers, the risk of a loss of asset value on investments in such assets as stocks, bonds, mortgages, and real estate.

C-2 risk (pricing risk). For insurers, the risk that an insurer's experience with mortality or expenses will differ significantly from the actuarial assumptions used in product pricing, causing the insurer to lose money on its products.

C-3 risk (interest-rate risk). For insurers, the risk that market interest rates might shift, causing an insurer's assets to lose value or its liabilities to gain value.

C-4 risk (general management risk). For insurers, the risk of losses resulting from the insurer's ineffective general business practices, from the need to pay a special assessment to cover another insurer's unsound business practices, from unfavorable regulatory changes, or from unfavorable changes in tax laws.

cafeteria plan. *See* **flexible benefits plan.**

calendar-year deductible. For medical expense insurance policies, an amount of eligible medical expenses that the insured must incur during a given calendar year (from January 1 to December 31) before the insurer becomes liable to pay any benefits for further covered expenses.

call center. Within a business organization, any group of individuals whose main function is to provide customer service by answering incoming customer calls or electronic mail messages that are routed through a computerized distribution system.

Canada Customs and Revenue Agency. The federal governmental agency responsible for enforcing the provisions of Canadian laws and regulations concerning income taxes.

Canada Health Act. In Canada, federal legislation that requires that each Canadian province provide its residents with health care coverage for hospital and medical services.

Canada Labour Code. Canadian federal legislation that mandates minimum wage and overtime standards that are similar to the standards established by the Fair Labor Standards Act in the United States.

Canada Pension Plan (CPP). A Canadian federal program that primarily provides retirement benefits for retirees who reside in all provinces except Quebec and who have contributed money into the plan during their working years. The program also provides a benefit to disabled workers, as well as to the widows, widowers, and surviving dependent children of deceased and disabled workers.

Canadian and British Insurance Companies Act. A Canadian federal statute that describes the requirements that federally incorporated Canadian insurers and British insurers must meet in order to transact business in Canada.

Canadian Council of Insurance Regulators (CCIR). In Canada, a committee of provincial superintendents of insurance that recommends uniform insurance legislation to the provinces.

Canadian Institute of Chartered Accountants (CICA). A professional organization of Canadian Chartered Accountants (CAA) that establishes generally accepted accounting principles (GAAP) for Canadian insurers to follow in recording and presenting their financial information.

Canadian Life and Health Insurance Association (CLHIA). An insurance industry association of life and health insurance companies operating in Canada.

Canadian Life and Health Insurance Compensation Corporation (CompCorp). In Canada, a federally incorporated, nonprofit company established by the Canadian Life and Health Insurance Association to protect insurance consumers against loss of benefits in the event a life or health insurance company becomes insolvent. Operates similarly to state guaranty associations. *See also* **guaranty association.**

Canadian Reinsurance Conference (CRC). An annual meeting of Canadian insurance companies and reinsurance companies that provides a forum for current life and health insurance and reinsurance issues. The CRC establishes the Canadian Reinsurance Guidelines.

Canadian Reinsurance Guidelines. A set of common reinsurance principles, established by the Canadian Reinsurance Conference (CRC), that can be voluntarily used as a basis upon which new reinsurance treaties can be written and existing treaties can be interpreted.

cancellable policy. An individual health insurance policy that gives the insurer the right to terminate the policy at any time, for any reason, simply by notifying the policyowner that the policy is cancelled and by refunding any advance premium paid for the policy. *See also* **conditionally renewable policy, noncancellable and guaranteed renewable policy,** and **optionally renewable policy.**

cap. For an equity-indexed annuity contract, the upper limit on the amount of an index's gain in value that will be credited to the annuity contract.

capacity. In insurance, the highest dollar amount of coverage that an insurer or reinsurer is financially able to accept on a specified risk.

capital. (1) An amount of money invested in a company by its owners, usually through the purchase of the company's stock. Also known as *owners' equity*. (2) Long-term funds.

capital and surplus. For insurers, the amount remaining after liabilities are subtracted from assets; owners' equity in an insurance company.

capital and surplus ratios. Financial ratios insurance companies use to express the relationship between the insurer's capital and/or surplus and its liabilities and thus to measure an insurer's financial strength. Also known as *capital ratios* and *capitalization ratios*.

capital appreciation. An increase in the market value of invested assets.

capital budget. A budget that shows a company's plans for the financial management of its long-term, high-cost investment proposals, such as new investments, major repairs to or remodeling of existing investments, acquisitions of other companies or lines of business, mandated safety and environmental improvements, expense reduction projects, and revenue expansion projects.

capital gain. The amount by which the selling price of an asset exceeds its purchase price. *Contrast with* **capital loss.**

capitalization ratios. *See* **capital and surplus ratios.**

capitalize. To record an expense, such as deferred acquisition costs, as an asset.

capital loss. The amount by which the purchase price of an asset exceeds its selling price. *Contrast with* **capital gain.**

capital ratios. *See* **capital and surplus ratios.**

capitation. A fee payment method used by some health maintenance organizations (HMOs) under which the HMO prepays a medical care provider a flat amount for each subscriber's medical care—usually on a monthly basis.

captive agent. An insurance agent who is under contract to only one insurer and who is not permitted to sell the products of other insurers. Also known as *exclusive agent. Contrast with* **broker.**

captive reinsurer. A reinsurance company that is formed and controlled by an insurance company or another type of insurance marketer for the purpose of providing reinsurance to that insurer or marketer.

career agency system. *See* **agency building distribution system.**

career agent. A licensed insurance salesperson who is under contract with at least one insurance company. A career agent is considered to be an independent contractor and not an employee of the insurance company.

caregiver training benefit. A benefit provided in a long-term care (LTC) policy to cover the cost of training someone to help care for a covered person who is to receive LTC at home or at an alternate living facility.

case assignment system. A system for organizing underwriting work in which cases are distributed to an appropriate person or group for underwriting based on certain characteristics of the case; for example, the face amount requested, the type of application of policy change, or the geographic origin of the application or location of the agent. *Contrast with* **work division system.**

case management. A process insurers use in managed health care plans to evaluate the necessity and quality of an insured's medical care and the appropriateness of alternative treatments or solutions for the insured's medical care.

cash-basis accounting. An accounting system in which a company recognizes revenues or expenses only when it receives or disburses cash.

cash budget. A type of budget that projects a company's beginning cash balance, cash inflows, cash outflows, and ending cash balance for a specified accounting period, typically by quarter.

cash disbursement. The payment of cash by a company.

cash disbursements budget. A schedule of expected cash disbursements, including their timing and amount, during the accounting period.

cash dividend option. For participating insurance policies, a dividend option under which the insurer sends the policyowner a check in the amount of the policy dividend. *See also* **dividend** and **policy dividend options**.

cash equivalents. Short-term assets that are not cash, but can typically be converted to cash within 90 days with little or no risk of losing value.

cash flow. Any movement of cash into or out of a company. A *cash inflow* is a source of funds and a *cash outflow* is a use of funds.

cash flow statement. A financial statement that provides information about an insurer's cash receipts (inflows) and its cash disbursements (outflows) during a specified period.

cash-flow testing (CFT). The use of simulation modeling to project into a future period the cash flows associated with an insurance company's existing business, as of a given valuation date, and to compare the timing and amounts of asset and liability cash flows after the valuation date. *Contrast with* **dynamic financial analysis (DFA)**.

cash inflow. *See* **cash flow.**

cash management. The management of short-term funds. Also known as *working capital management*.

cash-out provision. *See* **bailout provision**.

cash outflow. *See* **cash flow.**

cash payment option. One of several nonforfeiture options included in life insurance policies and some annuity contracts that allows a policyowner to receive the cash surrender value of a life insurance policy or an annuity contract in a single payment. Also known as *cash surrender option. See also* **nonforfeiture options** and **cash surrender value.**

cash receipt. A check, money order, electronic funds transfer (EFT), or other cash transaction that is remitted to a company as a form of payment for goods or services rendered.

cash receipts budget. A schedule of cash receipts expected during the specified accounting period.

cash surrender option. *See* **cash payment option** and **cash surrender value.**

cash surrender value. (1) For life insurance, the amount, before adjustments for factors such as policy loans, that the owner of a permanent life insurance policy is entitled to receive if the policy does not remain in force until the insured's death. (2) For annuities, the amount of a deferred annuity's accumulated value, less any surrender charges, that the contractholder is entitled to receive if the policy is surrendered during its accumulation period. Also known as *cash value* and *surrender value.*

cash value. *See* **cash surrender value.**

cash value accumulation test. For U.S. federal income tax purposes, one of the qualification tests an insurance policy must satisfy in order to be considered a life insurance contract that provides a tax-free death benefit. A policy passes this test if, according to the contract terms, the amount of its cash surrender value is never greater than the amount of net single premium needed to fund the policy death benefit.

casualty insurance. *See* **liability insurance.**

cat cover. *See* **catastrophe reinsurance.**

catastrophe reinsurance. A type of nonproportional reinsurance that protects a ceding company from multiple individual claims and/ or excessive losses resulting from a single event. Also known as *cat cover.*

CBO. *See* **collateralized bond obligation.**

CCIR. *See* **Canadian Council of Insurance Regulators.**

CCRC. *See* **continuing care retirement community.**

CD. *See* **certificate of deposit.**

CDS. *See* **Complaints Database System.**

CDSC. *See* **surrender charge.**

CDSL. *See* **surrender charge.**

cede. An insurance company's transfer of all or part of a specified risk to a reinsurance company.

ceding company. In a reinsurance transaction, the insurance company that purchases reinsurance to cover all or part of those risks that the insurer does not wish to retain in full. *Contrast with* **reinsurer.**

certificate holder. An individual who is insured under a group insurance contract and who has received a certificate of insurance. *See also* **certificate of insurance.**

certificate of authority. In the United States, a document issued by a state insurance department granting an insurer the right to conduct an insurance business in that state. Also known as *license.*

certificate of coverage. *See* **certificate of insurance.**

certificate of coverage provision. In the United States, a provision that most states require group life, health, and annuity policies to include which states that the insurer will issue a certificate to the policyholder for delivery to each person insured by the policy.

certificate of deposit (CD). A contractual agreement issued by a bank that returns the investor's principal with interest on a specified date.

certificate of incorporation. In the United States, a document issued by a state agency that grants a corporation its legal existence and right to operate as a corporation. Also known as *corporate charter. See also* **articles of incorporation.**

certificate of insurance. In group insurance, a document that a group policyholder delivers to each group insured which describes the coverage provided and the group insured's rights to insurance. Also known as *certificate of coverage. See also* **master contract.**

certificate of registry. In Canada, a document that is issued by the federal Minister of Finance and that grants an insurance company subject to federal regulation the right to transact business in Canada.

cession. Both the unit of insurance that an insurance company cedes to a reinsurer and the document used to record the transfer of risk from a ceding company to a reinsurer.

CFT. *See* **cash-flow testing.**

change in health statement. A statement contained in most individual life insurance applications and premium receipts that requires a proposed insured to notify the insurer in writing if her health or any material information in the application changes before the policy is delivered.

change of beneficiary provision. A provision included in individual life insurance policies and health insurance policies providing a death benefit that states the procedure the policyowner should follow for making a beneficiary change.

change of occupation provision. An individual disability income insurance policy provision that permits the insurer to adjust the policy's premium rate or the amount of benefits payable under the policy if the insured changes occupation.

chargeback. A method for allocating costs within an organization that allocates indirect costs to departments based on a department's usage.

children's insurance rider. A rider that may be added to a whole life insurance policy that provides term life insurance coverage on the insured's children.

chronically ill individual. Under the Health Insurance Portability and Accountability Act (HIPAA) in the United States, an insured person whom a licensed health care practitioner certifies as someone who is unable to perform, without substantial assistance, at least two activities of daily living (ADLs), or has a similar level of disability, or requires substantial supervision to protect themselves from threats to health or safety due to severe cognitive impairment. *See also* **activities of daily living (ADLs)**.

churning. An unethical and often illegal sales practice designed to increase commission sales. (1) In insurance sales, churning can occur when an agent induces a policyowner to cash in a policy and buy another, even though the replacement is not in the policyowner's best interest. *See also* **replacement**. (2) In stock and bond sales, churning can occur when a broker engages in excessive and unwarranted trading of clients' accounts.

CICA. *See* **Canadian Institute of Chartered Accountants**.

CI insurance. *See* **critical illness insurance**.

Civil Rights Act of 1964. In the United States, a federal anti-discrimination statute that applies to employers that are engaged in interstate commerce and that have 15 or more employees. Title VII of this act prohibits employers from discriminating in hiring, advancement, wages, and other terms and conditions of employment on the basis of sex, race, color, religion, or national origin.

claim. A request for payment of benefits under the terms of an insurance policy following the occurrence of a covered loss.

claim administration. Within an insurance company, the insurance administration function that assesses each claim made, decides whether the claim is justified, and authorizes the payment of benefits to the proper person.

claim analyst. *See* **claim examiner.**

claimant. A person who submits a claim to an insurance company.

claim approver. *See* **claim examiner.**

claim examiner. An insurance company employee who is responsible for processing and paying claims for policy benefits that the insurer receives. Also known as *claim approver, claim analyst,* and *claim specialist.*

claim fraud. An action by which a person intentionally uses false information in an unfair or unlawful attempt to collect benefits under an insurance policy.

claim investigation. The process an insurer undertakes to obtain additional information necessary to make a claim decision.

claim liabilities. *See* **policy and contract claims**.

claim philosophy. A precise statement of the principles an insurer will follow in conducting claim administration.

claim reserves. On an insurance company's financial statements, liabilities that identify the amounts that an insurer will pay in the future on claims already incurred but not paid in full as of the statement date. *See also* **disabled life reserves**.

claim settlement. A lump-sum payment by an insurer to a claimant in exchange for the claimant's agreement to release the insurer from further responsibility for coverage under the policy.

claim specialist. *See* **claim examiner.**

class beneficiary designation. A life insurance policy beneficiary designation that identifies the beneficiaries of the policy as members of a group—for example, "my children"—rather than naming each person individually.

class of policies. All policies of a particular type that an insurer has issued or all policies an insurer has issued to a particular group of insureds.

Clayton Act. U.S. federal antitrust law that makes it unlawful for businesses to engage in certain actions that are believed to lessen competition and to lead to monopolies.

CLHIA. *See* **Canadian Life and Health Insurance Association**.

CLHIA Guidelines. Recommendations to insurance companies adopted by the Canadian Life and Health Insurance Association

(CLHIA). Insurers are expected to abide by these guidelines as a condition of membership in the CLHIA.

closed contract. A contract for which only those terms and conditions that are printed in—or attached to—the contract are considered to be part of the contract. *Contrast with* **open contract.**

closed group valuation. An assessment of the value of a pension plan that takes into account only the benefits of persons currently affiliated with the plan as active participants, terminated vested participants, retired participants, or beneficiaries. Also known as *static valuation. Contrast with* **open group valuation.**

closed panel HMO. A type of health maintenance organization (HMO) that requires physicians either to belong to a group of physicians that has contracted with the HMO or to be employees of the HMO in order to provide services to HMO members. *Contrast with* **open panel HMO.**

closing. (1) In insurance sales, the part of an insurance sales presentation that occurs when an agent secures a purchase commitment from a prospect by asking for and obtaining the prospect's agreement to submit an application for the coverage recommended in the proposal. (2) Generally, a conclusion of a transaction, usually accomplished by satisfaction of all conditions stated in a purchase contract.

closing entry. An accounting entry that a company makes at the end of each accounting period to start the next accounting period with a zero balance in its temporary accounts.

CMO. *See* **collateralized mortgage obligation.**

COB provision. *See* **coordination of benefits provision.**

COBRA. *See* **Consolidated Omnibus Budget Reconciliation Act.**

COBRA continuation coverage. In the United States, group health insurance coverage provided to an individual who's employer-provided group health insurance has terminated because of certain qualifying events that are specified in the Consolidated Omnibus Budget Reconciliation Act (COBRA). *See also* **Consolidated Omnibus Budget Reconciliation Act (COBRA).**

cognitive impairment. In long-term care (LTC) insurance underwriting, mental incapacity that prevents a person from performing activities of daily living (ADLs) or from living safely. *See also* **activities of daily living (ADLs).**

cognitive reinstatement provision. A provision in a long-term care (LTC) insurance policy that permits reinstatement of the policy if the reason for the policy's lapse is that the policyholder has a cognitive impairment and that the reason for the missed premium payment was mental impairment.

coinsurance. (1) In medical expense insurance coverage, the percentage, usually 10 to 25 percent, of all eligible medical expenses, in excess of the deductible, that the insured is required to pay. Also known as *expense participation feature.* (2) In reinsurance, a type of proportional reinsurance in which an insurer and a reinsurer share the obligations of a policy, including paying the death benefit and the nonforfeiture values, and establishing the reserves.

coinsurance with funds withheld. A type of proportional reinsurance in which the ceding company retains funds that are due to the reinsurer, usually in an amount equal to the reserve required by law.

COLA benefit. *See* **cost-of-living increase benefit.**

cold calling. An insurance sales method in which an agent writes, calls, or visits prospects for insurance with whom he has had no prior contact. Also known as *cold canvassing.*

collateral assignment. A temporary transfer of some of the ownership rights in a particular property, such as a life insurance policy or an annuity contract, as collateral for a loan. The transfer is made on the condition that upon payment of the debt for which the contract is collateral, all transferred rights shall revert back to the original owner. *Contrast with* **absolute assignment.**

collateralized bond obligation (CBO). A type of bond that is secured by and represents a share in a portfolio of bond investments.

collateralized mortgage obligation (CMO). A type of bond that is secured by and represents a share in a portfolio of mortgage investments.

collision insurance. Insurance that covers an insured for losses to a vehicle caused by a collision regardless of whether the insured was at fault for the accident.

collusion. A secret agreement entered into by two or more persons to perpetrate an illegal act.

combination pension plan. A type of pension plan that uses both insured and uninsured funding. Also known as *split-funded plan*. *Contrast with* **trusteed pension plan** and **fully-insured pension plan**.

combined retention. *See* **corporate retention limit**.

commingling of funds. In insurance sales, the illegal practice of combining money belonging to policyowners with an agent's own funds.

commission. An amount of money paid to compensate a sales producer. For insurance sales, the amount is usually expressed as a percentage of the gross premiums paid by the insurance customer each year the policy is in force. For life insurance sales, the first-year commission is traditionally a higher percentage than the percentage commission paid in subsequent years. *See also* **deposit-based commission schedule**, **level commission schedule**, and **levelized commission schedule**.

committed cost. In accounting, a cost that results from a prior management decision and that cannot be changed quickly.

committee underwriting. A method used to organize underwriting work in which a committee of highly qualified people from inside and outside the underwriting function is called together for case assessment.

common cost. *See* **indirect cost**.

common disaster clause. A life insurance policy provision which states that the beneficiary must survive the insured by a specified period, such as 30 or 60 days, in order to receive the policy proceeds. Otherwise, the policy proceeds will be paid as though the beneficiary had died prior to the insured. Also known as *survivorship clause* and *time clause*.

common interest association. An association of individuals who share a common status or a common interest. Examples include associations of retired persons, gun owners, participants in a specific sport, or alumni of a specific college. Common interest associations typically are eligible for an association group insurance policy.

common stock. An equity asset that represents an ownership share in a corporation and that usually entitles the owner to vote on the selection of directors and on other important company matters and also entitles the owner to receive dividends on the stock. *Contrast with* **preferred stock**. *See also* **dividend** and **equity assets**.

community-property laws. In the United States, state laws, which provide that a spouse is entitled to receive an equal share of earned income and an equal share of property acquired by the other spouse during a marriage.

commutation right. The right granted by an insurer to an annuity contract owner to withdraw a lump sum from an annuity during the payout period. Any lump sum withdrawn reduces the dollar amount of future annuity payments.

commutative contract. An agreement under which the contracting parties specify the values that they will exchange; moreover, the parties generally exchange items or services that they think are of relatively equal value. *Contrast with* **aleatory contract.**

comparative financial statements. Financial statements that present a company's data for two or more accounting periods so that interested users can identify similarities and differences.

CompCorp. *See* **Canadian Life and Health Insurance Compensation Corporation.**

compensatory damages. In a lawsuit, an amount of money awarded to a plaintiff for the actual damage suffered from another's wrongdoing. *See also* **punitive damages.**

Competition Act of 1986. Canadian federal legislation designed to prevent undesirable monopolies, price fixing, and other anticompetitive or deceptive trade practices. In Canada, federally incorporated (registered) companies are subject to federal regulation.

complaint examiner. In the United States, a state insurance department employee who is responsible for handling complaints received from consumers about insurers.

Complaints Database System (CDS). In the United States, a database compiled and maintained by the National Association of Insurance Commissioners (NAIC) to provide state insurance regulators with aggregated complaint data on insurers across the country.

compliance. For insurers and their agents, the act of adhering to applicable laws and regulations that govern the operations of insurance companies.

compliance function. Within an insurance company, the area responsible for ensuring that all of the actions the insurer takes comply with applicable laws and regulatory requirements.

compound accounting entry. An accounting record of a financial transaction that affects more than two accounts.

compound interest. The type of interest that is earned on both the original principal amount and on the interest accumulated from earlier periods. *Contrast with* **simple interest.**

comprehensive budget. *See* **master budget.**

comprehensive personal liability insurance. Insurance that covers insureds from liability losses they incur that are not the result of practicing their profession or operating a vehicle.

comptroller. *See* **controller.**

concurrent review. A component of utilization review used by some health insurers whereby the utilization review organization monitors an insured's treatment and prognosis while he is in the hospital. *See also* **utilization review.**

conditional premium receipt. A type of premium receipt that specifies certain conditions that must be met before temporary insurance coverage provided by the receipt becomes effective.

conditionally renewable policy. An individual health insurance policy that gives the insurer a limited right to refuse to renew the policy at the end of a premium payment period for reasons specified in the policy. For example, a disability income policy might specify the continued employment of the insured, and a long-term care insurance policy might specify a maximum age limit. *See also* **cancellable policy, noncancellable and guaranteed renewable policy,** and **optionally renewable policy.**

confirmation statement. *See* **transaction confirmation.**

conflict of laws. The area of law that determines which substantive laws apply to each issue in a case when the laws of more than one jurisdiction are involved in the action.

conformity with state statutes provision. In the United States, an individual health insurance policy provision which states that any policy provision in conflict with the laws of the state in which the insured resides is amended to conform to the minimum requirements of such laws.

conservation. In the insurance industry, an insurer's efforts to ensure that insurance policies and annuities, once issued, do not lapse but are retained on the insurer's books for as long as possible.

conservation unit. Within an insurance company, a group of employees dedicated to promoting conservation of policies.

conservative financial strategy. A financial management strategy that avoids risks and places an unusually strong emphasis on company solvency.

conservative mortality table. A mortality table with a mortality safety margin built into its rates. For annuities, a conservative mortality table shows lower mortality rates than the expected mortality rates. For life insurance policies, a conservative mortality table shows higher mortality rates than the expected mortality rates.

conservator. *See* receiver.

conservatorship. *See* receivership.

consideration. One of the requirements for the formation of a valid informal contract that is met when each party gives or promises to give something of value to the other party.

Consolidated Omnibus Budget Reconciliation Act (COBRA). A U.S. federal law that generally applies to employers with 20 or more employees and requires each group medical expense insurance plan to allow employees and certain dependents to continue their group coverage for a stated period of time following a qualifying event that causes the loss of group medical expense coverage.

constructive delivery of a policy. An insurance policy delivery that occurs when an insurer releases the policy with intent to be bound by it regardless of whether the policy is physically delivered to the applicant. For example, courts have found that constructive delivery occurs when a policy is mailed to an authorized agent of the insurer.

consultant. According to the Agents and Brokers Licensing Model Act in the United States, an individual, partnership, or corporation that, for a fee, offers advice, counsel, opinion, or service with respect to the benefits, advantages, or disadvantages promised under any insurance policy that could be issued in the state.

consumer credit insurance. Credit insurance that is subject to the requirements of the Consumer Credit Insurance Model Act, including credit life insurance, credit accident and health insurance, and credit unemployment insurance.

Consumer Credit Insurance Model Act. In the United States, a National Association of Insurance Commissioners (NAIC) model law that regulates consumer credit insurance issued or sold in connection with loans or other credit transactions for personal, family, or household purposes.

consumer credit report. Any communication of information by a consumer reporting agency that bears on a consumer's credit worthiness, credit standing, credit capacity, character, general reputation, personal characteristics, or mode of living and is obtained directly from the consumer's creditors or from the consumer. Also known as *consumer report.*

consumer protection agency. In the United States, an agency within a state that is responsible for enforcing the state's consumer protection laws.

consumer report. *See* **consumer credit report.**

consumer reporting agency. Any party that regularly assembles or evaluates consumer credit information or other information on consumers, either for profit or on a cooperative, nonprofit basis, for the purpose of furnishing consumer credit reports to other people and organizations.

contest. To dispute the validity of a contract.

contestable period. The time during which an insurer has the right to cancel or rescind an insurance policy if the application contained a material misrepresentation. *See also* **incontestability provision.**

contingency. (1) An exposure to risk. (2) For an insurance company, an unexpected event that causes the insurer's actual expenses, investment earnings, mortality rates, or persistency rates to deviate significantly from company assumptions.

contingency allowance. An amount built in to an insurance product's price to offset the possibility that unexpected events—such as greater-than-anticipated mortality rates, earthquakes, epidemics, or declines in expected investment earnings—may adversely affect a product's profit margin.

contingency reserve. A voluntary, noncontractual reserve established by an insurer to supply added reserve protection against various special categories of risk, usually related to the C-1 through C-4 risks. *See also* **special surplus.**

contingency risks. *See* **C risks.**

contingent annuitant. A person who would become the annuitant if the primary annuitant were to die during the accumulation period of an annuity whose contract owner and annuitant are two different persons. *See also* **annuitant.**

contingent beneficiary. The party designated to receive the proceeds of a life insurance policy following the insured's death if the primary beneficiary predeceased the insured. Also known as *secondary beneficiary* and *successor beneficiary*. *See also* **primary beneficiary.**

contingent deferred sales charge (CDSC). *See* **contingent deferred sales load (CDSL).**

contingent deferred sales load (CDSL). In variable life insurance or annuity products, a one-time charge potentially deducted from withdrawals and applied for recovery of sales expenses. Also known as *contingent deferred sales charge* (CDSC). *See also* **surrender charge.**

contingent payee. (1) For life insurance, the person or party who is to receive insurance policy proceeds in accordance with the terms of a settlement agreement following the payee's death. Also known as *successor payee*. (2) For annuity contracts, a person designated by the annuity contract owner to receive any remaining annuity payments upon the death of the payee.

continuing care retirement community (CCRC). For long-term care (LTC) insurance, a type of assisted living facility that provides both separate housing and living arrangements of the boarding-house type. Residents contract with the community for LTC services.

continuous-premium whole life insurance policy. A whole life insurance policy for which premiums are payable until the insured's death. Also known as *straight life insurance policy* and *ordinary life insurance policy*.

contra account. In accounting, an account that accompanies a specified "companion" account—typically an asset account—and that has a normal balance that is the opposite of the companion account.

contract. A legally enforceable agreement between two or more parties. For an insurance or annuity product, the document that describes the legally binding agreement between the insurance company and the contract owner.

contract fee. *See* **administrative fee.**

contract form filing. In insurance, the process of contacting all appropriate regulatory jurisdictions and meeting their requirements in order to obtain clearance to sell a given product in that jurisdiction.

contractholder. *See* **contract owner.**

contract law. A body of law that governs the requirements for forming a legally binding contract and that specifies the rights and duties of the parties to the contract.

contract of adhesion. A contract that one contracting party prepares and that the other contracting party must accept or reject as a whole, without any bargaining between the parties. Insurance contracts are contracts of adhesion.

contract of indemnity. An insurance policy under which the amount of the policy benefit payable for a covered loss is based on the actual amount of financial loss as determined at the time of loss. For example, many medical expense policies are contracts of indemnity. *Contrast with* **valued contract.**

contract owner. The individual or entity who applies for, purchases, and owns a life insurance or an annuity contract. For an annuity, the contract owner usually is also the annuitant. Also known as *contractholder.*

contract summary. For an annuity, a document that identifies and describes the features of a specific annuity that a consumer is considering purchasing.

contractual reserve. *See* **policy reserve.**

contractual savings institution. A financial institution, such as an insurance company, that acquires funds at periodic intervals on a contractual basis.

contribution margin. When pricing a product, the difference between the product's selling price and its variable costs.

contribution to surplus. In a mutual insurance company, the excess of revenues over expenses before payment of policy dividends.

contributory plan. (1) A group insurance plan under which individual group members must contribute some or all of the premium in order to be covered under the group plan. (2) A retirement plan that requires plan participants to make contributions to fund the plan. *Contrast with* **noncontributory plan.**

controller. The head of a company's accounting function. Also known as *comptroller*.

conversion provision. A provision sometimes included in individual insurance policies or group insurance policies that allows the policyowner or insured group member to change from one type of insurance coverage to another in certain prescribed situations without presenting evidence that the insured is an insurable risk. (1) In individual term life insurance policies, the provision allows the policyowner to convert the term policy to a permanent plan of insurance. (2) In group life insurance, the provision allows a group insured whose coverage terminates for certain reasons to convert the group coverage to an individual policy of insurance. (3) For group long-term care insurance, the provision allows the group member leaving the group to convert the group coverage to an individual policy. Also known as *conversion privilege* and *conversion feature*.

convertible term insurance policy. A term life insurance policy that gives the policyowner the right to convert the policy to a permanent plan of insurance.

coordination of benefits (COB) provision. A provision in group medical expense plans that prevents duplicate benefit payments for the same expense by more than one insurer or by a government program and that defines the order in which the involved groups are to pay benefits. The purpose of the COB provision is to assure that an insured does not receive benefit amounts greater than his or her actual incurred medical expenses. *See also* **overinsurance provision**.

copayment. (1) For medical expense insurance plans, a portion of an insured's medical costs that must be paid by the insured as a condition of the insurer paying the remaining portion. (2) For health maintenance organizations (HMOs), a fee imposed on HMO subscribers each time they receive specified medical services.

corporate bonds. Bonds issued by a corporation.

corporate budget. *See* **master budget**.

corporate charter. *See* **certificate of incorporation**.

corporate retention limit. In reinsurance, the maximum amount of risk that a group of affiliated companies will retain on any one life. Also known as *combined retention*.

corporation. A legal entity that exists separately from its owners and that can enter into contracts, sue in court or be sued, own property, and engage in other business transactions.

correspondent. For a particular group insurance plan, the person in the policyholder's organization who serves as liaison with the insurer.

corridor. In reinsurance, an amount above the ceding company's retention limit that a risk must meet or exceed before any part of the risk is ceded to a reinsurer. The purpose of the corridor is for the ceding company to avoid ceding small amounts of coverage.

cost accounting. An accounting system for accumulating expense data that is used to facilitate effective cost control and to make accurate estimates of future costs for use in the pricing of a company's products.

cost allocation. The accounting process of assigning or distributing an indirect cost (expense) according to a specified method or formula. Also known as *expense allocation.*

cost basis. In insurance, the price paid for an insurance or annuity contract. (1) For an insurance contract, the sum of the net premiums paid, plus accumulated dividends, minus certain specified costs. (2) For an annuity contract, the portion of the annuity's accumulated value on which income tax has already been paid.

cost center. A department or other segment of a business organization to which costs (expenses) can be traced.

cost comparison indexes. In individual life insurance sales, calculations by which to derive a cost figure for an individual life insurance policy. By comparing the index numbers derived for similar policies, a consumer has some basis on which to compare the costs of the policies.

cost concept. An accounting principle which states that companies should include items on the balance sheet and income statement according to their actual cost at the time of purchase. Also known as *acquisition-cost concept.*

cost object. Any purpose for which a company measures costs.

cost of benefits. The value of all contractually required benefits that a life insurance or an annuity product promises to pay.

cost-of-living adjustment (COLA) benefit. *See* cost-of-living increase benefit.

cost-of-living increase benefit. A disability income policy benefit that provides for periodic increases in the disability income benefit amount being paid to a disabled insured to compensate for an increase in the cost of living. Also known as *cost-of-living adjustment (COLA) benefit.*

cost recovery rule. (1) For annuities, a U.S. federal income tax rule stating that amounts withdrawn from an annuity are considered to be a return of the owner's cost basis first and, thus, are non-taxable to the extent total amounts withdrawn do not exceed the cost basis. (2) For life insurance surrenders, a U.S. federal income tax rule under which a policyowner who receives the surrender value of a life insurance policy in a lump-sum payment is taxed on the amount of any gain realized from the surrender.

cost-volume-profit (CVP) analysis. The study of the effects of changes in product prices, sales volume, fixed costs, variable costs, and the type of products a company offers. Also known as *breakeven analysis.*

coupon advertisement. According to Canadian insurance regulations, (1) a sales inducement designed to invite the public to contract for insurance by the inclusion of an application for an individual insurance contract or (2) a broad description of coverage designed to invite the public to request an application for insurance with additional printed material for the purpose of issuing the applicant an individual insurance contract.

CPP. *See* **Canada Pension Plan.**

CPT. *See* **Physicians' Current Procedural Terminology.**

CRC. *See* **Canadian Reinsurance Conference.**

credibility factor. In using blended rating to calculate premium rates for group insurance, a percentage that represents the amount of weight given to a group's actual claim experience.

credit. A specified change made to the monetary value of a financial account. A credit increases the value of liability accounts, owners' equity accounts, and revenue accounts, whereas it decreases the value of asset accounts and expense accounts.

credit accident and health insurance. *See* **credit insurance.**

credit card. An open-ended credit arrangement in which a lender agrees to pay for goods and services purchased by a consumer and the consumer repays the lender in monthly payments at a specified rate of interest on the amount of the monthly outstanding balance.

Credit for Reinsurance Model Law. A National Association of Insurance Commissioners (NAIC) model law that specifies the situations in which an insurer is entitled to reinsurance reserve credits.

credit insurance. Insurance that pays a benefit equal to part or all of the amount of unpaid debt under a credit transaction if the insured borrower dies or becomes disabled.

credit risk. The possibility of poor financial performance on the part of a business; also, the possibility that a borrower (an individual or a business) could be late with payments or could entirely fail to pay its obligations. Also known as *default risk.*

credit unemployment insurance. Insurance that provides funds for the payment of amounts due under a specific credit transaction while the insured debtor is involuntarily unemployed.

credit union group. A type of group that generally is eligible for group insurance coverage and that consists of members of a credit union.

creditable coverage. For purposes of the Health Insurance Portability and Accountability Act (HIPAA) in the United States, coverage of an individual under a group health plan or other specified health insurance coverage without a lapse of 63 days or more.

crediting rate. For a fixed annuity contract, the interest rate applied to a customer's accumulation value.

creditor group insurance. A type of business insurance designed to pay for the economic loss suffered by a creditor when one of its borrowers dies before the debt is repaid. The group policy is issued to the creditor and insures the lives of its debtors.

credits. In the numerical rating system used for underwriting life insurance, an applicant's medical, personal, and financial characteristics that have a favorable effect on the individual's mortality rating and are assigned "minus" values. *See also* **debits** and **numerical rating system.**

critical illness (CI) insurance. A type of individual health insurance that pays a lump-sum benefit when the insured is diagnosed with a specified illness. Also known as *critical diagnosis insurance*. *Contrast with* specified disease coverage.

cross-purchase method. A method of carrying out a partnership buy-sell agreement under which each partner agrees to purchase a proportionate share of a deceased partner's interest in the partnership. *Contrast with* entity method.

cross-selling. Identifying a customer's needs for additional financial products while selling a primary financial product.

CSR. *See* customer service representative.

cumulative dividends. A type of preferred stock dividend arrangement in which a company must pay in full any unpaid scheduled dividends on its preferred stock before it may pay any dividends on its common stock. *See also* common stock and preferred stock.

currency risk. The risk arising from changes in currency exchange rates.

current assets. *See* short-term assets.

current assumption whole life insurance. *See* interest-sensitive insurance.

current interest rate. (1) For an annuity contract, the interest rate, based on the prevailing interest rates in the economy when the annuity is purchased, that an insurer promises to pay for a specified time period—usually one, three, or five years. (2) Generally, the prevailing interest rate in the economy at a given time.

currently payable scale. As defined by the National Association of Insurance Commissioners (NAIC) Life Insurance Illustrations Model Regulation, a scale of nonguaranteed elements in effect for a policy on the date the illustration is prepared or declared to become effective within the next 95 days.

current market value. The price at which an asset can be sold under current economic conditions. Also known as *fair market value*.

current mortality rate. In a universal life (UL) insurance policy, the monthly mortality rate actually used to calculate the monthly mortality charge. This amount is generally substantially lower than the guaranteed maximum mortality rate. *See also* mortality rate.

current open claimants. For a particular group insurance plan, group members who are receiving short-term or long-term disability income benefits.

current ratio. A ratio that divides a company's current assets by its current liabilities to measure its short-term debt-paying ability.

custodial care. In long-term care (LTC) insurance, care that is largely of a non-medical nature, in which a patient receives assistance with activities of daily living provided by nurses or other qualified persons at a nursing home or a similar facility.

customer service. The broad range of activities that a company and its employees undertake in order to keep customers satisfied so they will continue doing business with the company and speak positively about the company to other potential customers.

customer service representative (CSR). Any person, other than a sales person, who provides support to customers face-to-face or through communications media.

CVP analysis. *See* **cost-volume-profit analysis.**

DA contract. *See* **deposit administration contract.**

DAC. *See* **deferred acquisition costs.**

daily benefit amount. Under a long-term care (LTC) insurance policy, the amount an insurer will pay for each day of an insured's long-term care at a care facility or in the insured's home.

data integrity check. A periodic review of electronic data to determine if the data has been duplicated, deleted, or incorrectly linked in an organization's various databases.

date of expiry. In reinsurance arrangements, the date upon which the reservation of reinsurance facilities will be cancelled if the reinsurer does not receive a cession or placement information from the ceding company.

DCAT. *See* **dynamic capital adequacy testing.**

dealer. A person or entity engaged in the business of buying or selling securities for its own account. *Contrast with* **broker.**

death benefit. (1) For a life insurance contract, the amount of money paid by an insurer to a beneficiary when a person insured under the life insurance policy dies. (2) For an annuity contract, the amount of money paid to a beneficiary if the contract owner dies before the annuity payments begin.

death certificate. A document that attests to the death of a person and that bears the signature—and sometimes the seal—of an official authorized to issue such a certificate.

death claim. A request for payment, upon the death of the insured, under the terms and conditions of a life insurance policy.

debenture. An unsecured corporate bond for which the borrower does not pledge any assets or income as security.

debit. (1) In accounting, a specified change made to the monetary value of an account. A debit increases the value of asset accounts and expense accounts, whereas it decreases the value of liability accounts, owners' equity accounts, and revenue accounts. (2) In the home service insurance distribution system, a group of clients or the geographical area to which a home service agent is assigned.

debit agent. *See* **home service agent.**

debit insurance. *See* **industrial insurance.** *See also* **home service distribution system.**

debits. In the numerical rating system used for underwriting life insurance, a proposed insured's medical, personal, and financial characteristics that have an unfavorable effect on the individual's mortality rating and are assigned "plus" values. *See also* **credits** and **numerical rating system.**

debt. An amount owed.

debt assets. Assets that represent an investor's loan of funds to a debtor in return for a promised repayment of the loan plus interest.

debtor-creditor group. A type of group that generally is eligible for group insurance and that consists of individuals who have borrowed money from a specific lender or lenders.

debt-to-equity ratio. A financial ratio, calculated by dividing a company's total long-term debt by its total equity, that is helpful in determining a company's solvency.

declined risk class. In insurance underwriting, the group of proposed insureds whose impairments or anticipated extra mortality are so great that an insurer cannot provide insurance coverage to them at an affordable cost. Also known as *uninsurable class. Contrast with* **preferred risk class, standard risk class,** and **substandard risk class.**

decreasing term life insurance. Term life insurance that provides a death benefit that decreases in amount over the policy term. *Contrast with* **increasing term life insurance.**

deductible. A feature included in a medical expense insurance policy that requires the insured to pay a flat dollar amount for eligible medical expenses before the insurer will begin making benefit payments under the policy.

deemer provision. In the United States, a regulatory provision which states that, if a state insurance department has not disapproved a policy form within a specified time—such as 30, 45, or 60 days from the date of filing, then the policy form is deemed to have been approved by the department.

default. A failure to meet a financial obligation.

default risk. *See* **credit risk.**

deferred acquisition costs (DAC). Costs reported under U.S. GAAP that are related primarily and directly to acquiring new business and retaining current business associated with new insurance products. Insurers establish a *deferred acquisition costs (DAC) account* in order to counterbalance the accounting entries for the amortization of first-year acquisition expenses.

deferred annuity. An annuity in which the benefit payments are scheduled to begin at some stated point in the future. *Contrast with* **immediate annuity.** *See also* **annuity certain, annuity due, ordinary annuity,** and **straight life annuity.**

deferred compensation plan. A plan established by an employer to provide income benefits to an employee at a later date, such as after the employee's retirement, if the employee does not voluntarily terminate employment before that date.

deferred policy acquisition costs (DPAC). *See* **deferred acquisition costs (DAC).**

deferred premiums. In the United States, life insurance premiums due after the date of the Annual Statement but before the next policy anniversary date and the next Annual Statement date.

deferred profit sharing plan (DPSP). A Canadian retirement program under which plan sponsor contributions are related to the sponsor's profits and are tax deductible by the plan sponsor, subject to specified annual maximum amounts.

defined benefit pension plan. A pension plan that identifies the amount of the retirement benefit each plan participant will receive at retirement. The amount of the benefit is based on the employee's income, years of service, or both income and years of service. The plan sponsor is obligated to deposit enough assets into the plan to provide the promised benefits. *Contrast with* **defined contribution pension plan.**

defined contribution pension plan. A pension plan that describes the plan sponsor's annual contribution to the plan on behalf of each plan participant. At retirement, the amount of a participant's benefit is calculated based on the accumulated value of contributions made by, or on behalf of, the participant. Also known as *money purchase plan*. *Contrast with* **defined benefit pension plan.**

demutualization. The process of converting a mutual insurance company's corporate form of organization to that of a stock insurance company. *See also* **mutual insurance company, mutualization,** and **stock insurance company.**

dental expense coverage. Supplemental medical expense insurance that provides benefits for routine dental examinations, preventive work, and dental procedures needed to treat tooth decay and diseases of the teeth and jaw.

dependent. For insurance purposes, a spouse or an unmarried child—including an adopted child, stepchild, or foster child—who is under age 19 or to age 25 if disabled or a full-time student, and who relies on an insured person for support and maintenance.

dependent life insurance. *See* **family benefit coverage.**

deposit administration (DA) contract. A funding vehicle for a pension plan in which the plan sponsor deposits assets with an insurer and the assets are placed in the insurer's general investment account. At a plan participant's retirement, the insurer withdraws funds from the general account to purchase an immediate annuity for the retiree. The insurer usually provides the plan sponsor with guarantees against investment loss, as well as a guaranteed minimum investment return. *See also* **immediate participation guarantee (IPG) contract.**

deposit-based commission schedule. A commission schedule for annuity sales agents in which the commissions are calculated as a percentage of new premiums paid into an annuity.

depository institution. A financial services company, such as a commercial bank or thrift institution, that engages in the retail banking activities of accepting deposits from individuals and making loans.

depreciation. In accounting, the systematic cost allocation process used to record the decline over time in the usefulness of a company's tangible assets. In general, a decline in price or value.

derivative. A financial security, such as a stock option, that derives its investment value from another security.

desk audit. In reinsurance, the systematic review of a ceding company's quality of administration, performed by the assuming company at the assuming company's offices.

desk examination. A state insurance department examination of some of an insurer's business records that is conducted in the offices of the insurance department.

determination letter. A letter issued by the Internal Revenue Service (IRS) in the United States in response to an insurer's request that the IRS evaluate a specific product and determine whether the product meets federal tax requirements.

development expenses. The expenses related to starting a new product or line of business.

DFA. *See* **dynamic financial analysis.**

diagnostic and treatment codes. Numbers and words that represent specific medical diagnoses and treatments and are used by health care providers to communicate medical information about medical expense claims to insurers. *See also* **International Classification of Diseases and Related Health Problems** and **Physicians' Current Procedural Terminology.**

Diagnostic Related Groups (DRGs). A medical expense claim payment method under which an insurer pays hospital charges not according to the number and types of services delivered, but according to the diagnosis for a patient.

DI insurance. *See* **disability income insurance.**

direct accounting method. A method of allocating organizational costs, which assumes that, a service department benefits production departments only.

direct contract HMO. A type of open panel health maintenance organization (HMO) that contracts directly with physicians to provide medical services for HMO members. *See also* **open panel HMO.**

direct cost. In accounting, a cost incurred for or physically traceable to one specific product, line of business, department, or other cost object. *Contrast with* **indirect cost.**

directed deposit. For a variable annuity contract, contributions made by the owner that specifically indicate the percentage of the deposit to be allocated to each investment subaccount.

director of insurance. *See* **insurance commissioner.**

direct response distribution system. An insurance sales distribution system wherein the customer purchases products directly from an insurer without the assistance of an insurance agent. The customer responds to the company's advertisements or telephone solicitations that are designed to elicit an immediate and measurable action—such as an inquiry or purchase—from the customer.

direct response product. In the insurance industry, an insurance product sold to consumers without the help of a marketer, usually through direct mail, advertising in print and other media, telephone solicitation, or, the Internet.

direct rollover. *See* **rollover.**

direct transfer. *See* **rollover.**

direct writer. *See* **direct writing company.**

direct writing company. An insurer that sells coverage directly to consumers. Also known as *direct writer* and *direct insurer*.

disability. In disability insurance, the inability of an insured person to work due to an injury or sickness. Each disability policy has a definition of disability that must be satisfied in order for the insured to receive the policy's benefits. *See also* **residual disability** and **total disability**.

disability buyout coverage. A type of disability income insurance that provides benefits designed to fund the buyout of a disabled partner or disabled owner in a business.

disability income insurance. A type of health insurance designed to compensate an insured person for a portion of the income lost because of a disabling injury or illness. Benefit payments are made either weekly or monthly for a specified period during the continuance of an insured's disability. *See also* **income protection insurance.**

disabled life reserves. For an insurance company, a claim reserve liability that is the present value of all amounts that are predicted to become payable while an insured is disabled. *See also* **claim reserves.**

disbursements. (1) In general usage, any payments of money. (2) For annuity contracts, payments insurers make from deferred annuity contracts during the accumulation period. Also known as *distributions.*

disciplined current scale. As defined by the National Association of Insurance Commissioners (NAIC) Life Insurance Illustrations Model Regulation, a scale of nonguaranteed elements that is based on an insurer's actual recent experience and that is certified by an illustration actuary. *See also* **illustration actuary.**

disclaimer (denial) of opinion. An auditor's statement indicating that an external auditor of an entity's financial statements has no opinion on the entity's financial statements.

disclosure. In marketing, the practice of providing consumers with specific types of information designed to improve purchasers' knowledge of the products they are considering purchasing and to enable them to compare the costs of various products.

disclosure statement. For individual retirement annuities, a written statement that an insurer in the United States must provide to consumers considering the purchase of an individual retirement annuity that provides nontechnical explanations of the operation of the annuity, including explanations of the statutory require-ments for such an annuity, the income tax consequences of purchasing such an annuity, and the income tax consequences of specific types of transactions relating to the annuity.

discount bond. A bond that has a current market value that is lower than the bond's principal or par value. *Contrast with* **premium bond.**

discounted fee-for-service payment structure. A fee structure used by some health maintenance organizations (HMOs) under which the HMO pays physicians a certain percentage of their normal fees, thereby achieving a "discount" on those fees.

discretionary costs. Costs that are partially or wholly under the control of current management and are flexible components of a budget that can be changed as conditions change.

discretionary group. According to the National Association of Insurance Commissioners (NAIC) Group Life Insurance and Group Health Insurance Standard Provisions Model Acts, any type of group other than a single employer group, a debtor-creditor group, a labor union group, a multiple employer group, an association group, or a credit union group that is eligible for group insurance if approved by the applicable state insurance department.

disintermediation. A phenomenon in which customers remove money from a financial intermediary. *See also* **run on assets.**

disputed claims. *See* **resisted claims.**

distribution. For sales operations, the process of transferring goods or services to customers.

distribution channel. *See* **distribution system.**

distribution expenses. All the costs directly associated with selling products. Insurance distribution expenses include agent compensation, group sales representatives' salaries, postal, printing, and telecommunications expenses.

distributions. *See* **disbursements.**

distribution system. In marketing, a network of organizations and individuals that performs all distribution activities. Also known as *distribution channel. See also* **distribution.**

district manager. For sales operations, an individual assigned to oversee the marketing operations for a company in a defined district within an overall sales area.

diversification. A defensive principle of investment portfolio construction that requires balancing the selection of portfolio assets among a variety of types of securities or industries.

dividend. (1) For investments, a share of a company's earnings that the company pays to the owners of its stock. Dividends paid in cash are called *cash dividends.* Dividends paid in the form of additional shares of stock are called *stock dividends.* (2) For participating insurance policies, a portion of an insurer's surplus paid to the owner of an individual participating life or annuity policy. Commonly referred to as a *policy dividend.* (3) For group insurance policies, a premium refund paid to the policyholder of a group insurance policy. *See also* **experience refund.**

dividend accumulations option. *See* **accumulation at interest option.**

dividend additions. *See* **paid-up additional insurance option.**

dividend provision. A provision included in participating life insurance and annuity contracts that describes the contract owner's right to share in the insurer's divisible surplus and the dividend payment options available to the contract owner. *See also* **policy dividend options.**

divisible surplus. The portion of an insurance company's earnings that is available for distribution to owners of the company's participating policies after deductions are made for liabilities, capital, and special surplus. Also known as *unassigned surplus. See also* **surplus.**

doctrine of reasonable expectations. In the field of insurance, a legal doctrine by which a court interprets the terms of any insurance contract in such a way as to honor the reasonable expectations of the individual who purchased the policy even though the language of the policy does not literally support these expectations.

dollar cost averaging. An investment strategy that involves investing a fixed dollar amount at regular intervals in one or more financial instruments.

domestic corporation. From the point of view of a particular state in the United States, a company that is incorporated under the laws of that state. *Contrast with* **alien corporation.**

domicile. *See* **state of domicile.**

domiciliary state. *See* **state of domicile.**

double indemnity benefit. An accidental death benefit that is equal to the face amount of a life insurance policy's basic death benefit and is paid when the insured's death is the result of an accident as defined in the policy. *See also* **accidental death benefit (ADB).**

DPAC. *See* **deferred acquisition costs (DAC).**

DPSP. *See* **deferred profit sharing plan.**

dread disease coverage. *See* **specified disease coverage.**

DRGs. *See* **Diagnostic Related Groups.**

drop letter. In reinsurance transactions, a written notice to a ceding company indicating that, if no response is received within a certain period of time—such as two weeks—the reinsurer will cancel the reservation of facilities.

drop notice. In reinsurance transactions, written notification to a reinsurer stating that a ceding company no longer needs the reinsurance and asking the reinsurer to cancel the reservation.

DST. *See* **dynamic solvency testing.**

dual accounting concept. An accounting concept that states that every financial transaction has two aspects—debits and credits—that always equal each other.

due and unpaid claims. Insurance claims that have been approved by an insurer but have not yet been paid to the policy beneficiary.

due diligence. An investigation process, required for merger agreements and reinsurance arrangements, which includes evaluating whether the investigated company (1) has adequate reserves and (2) uses sound pricing techniques.

due diligence review. *See* **external audit.**

due income. Income that was expected before a financial reporting date but that has not yet been received as of the reporting date.

dynamic analysis of financial condition. *See* **dynamic solvency testing (DST).**

dynamic budget. *See* **flexible budget.**

dynamic capital adequacy testing (DCAT). A type of scenario analysis required annually for insurers in Canada that employs simulation modeling to project, as of a given valuation date, the insurer's existing and future business, and to compare the amounts of the insurer's assets, liabilities, and owners' equity at various times after the valuation date. *See also* **scenario analysis.**

dynamic financial analysis (DFA). A form of scenario analysis, broader in scope than cash-flow testing, in which insurers use simulation modeling and multiple-scenario testing to project future values for an insurer's assets, liabilities, and owners' equity. *See also* **scenario analysis.**

dynamic valuation. *See* **open group valuation.**

E&O insurance. *See* **errors and omissions insurance.**

early retirement. The election by an eligible participant in a pension plan, to begin receiving plan benefits before the normal retirement age, subject to minimum age and service requirements and subject to a reduced pension income benefit.

early-warning financial ratio tests. A set of financial ratios that Canadian regulatory examiners use to analyze an insurer's financial statements and to create a customized examination plan that is designed to focus the on-site regulatory examination on the risks identified from the insurer's financial information.

earmarked surplus. *See* **special surplus.**

earnings. (1) Profits that are made through either labor or increases in the value of investments. (2) For an annuity, the amount that an annuity has increased in value above the purchase price.

earnings first rule. *See* **interest first rule.**

ECCF. *See* **extended congregate care facility.**

EDI. *See* **electronic data interchange.**

effective interest rate. Interest rate or rate of return that includes the effects of compounding. Also known as the *annual percentage rate (APR). Contrast with* **nominal interest rate.** *See also* **interest rate.**

effective yield. *See* **effective rate of return.**

EFT. *See* **electronic funds transfer.**

election period. For the purposes of the Consolidated Omnibus Budget Reconciliation Act (COBRA) in the United States, a specified period following a qualifying event during which a qualified beneficiary has the right to elect COBRA continuation health coverage. *See also* **Consolidated Omnibus Budget Reconciliation Act (COBRA), qualified beneficiaries,** and **qualifying events.**

electronic application submission. Insurance and annuity application process in which the sales agent or applicant enters the application information into a computer and the information is then transmitted over a data network directly to the insurer.

electronic data interchange (EDI). A computer-to-computer information exchange that uses a more uniform format than is used for much remote computing. EDI is neither company-specific nor company-owned, but is a public standard for electronic movement of data.

electronic funds transfer (EFT). A method of transferring funds between financial intermediaries through an electronic computer network.

eligibility period. In contributory group insurance plans, a specified time, usually 31 days, during which a new group member who is eligible for group insurance coverage may first enroll for that coverage, usually without having to provide evidence of insurability. Also known as *enrollment period.*

eligibility requirements. The conditions a person must satisfy in order to be a participant in a group life insurance, group health insurance, or group retirement plan. *See also* **service requirement.**

eligible employee. (1) Any employee of a sponsoring organization that satisfies certain qualifications for participation in the company's group life insurance, group health insurance, or group retirement plan. (2) According to the U.S. federal Family and Medical Leave Act, an employee who has been employed by a covered employer for at least 12 months and who has worked at least 1,250 hours during the 12 months preceding the start of a leave.

eligible individual. For purposes of the Health Insurance Portability and Accountability Act (HIPAA) in the United States, an individual to whom an insurer must provide individual health insurance coverage because the individual has had group health insurance coverage that meets specified requirements.

elimination period. (1) Under a disability income policy, the specific amount of time an insured must be disabled before becoming eligible to receive policy benefits. In a residual disability income policy, often referred to as a *qualification period*. (2) Under a long-term care policy, the number of days after long-term care begins that an insured must wait before benefit payments begin. Also known as *waiting period*.

employee benefits. The programs and services an employer offers to an employee in addition to regular monetary payments for work performed.

employee census. In group insurance, an attachment to a Request for Proposal that lists demographic information about the proposed group as a unit and about individual members within the group. *See also* **Request for Proposal**.

employee class. In group insurance, a group of employees categorized by position, earnings, or rank.

Employee Retirement Income Security Act (ERISA). A U.S. federal law that regulates both employee welfare benefit plans, including group life and health insurance plans established by employers, and employer-sponsored retirement plans. ERISA requires that such plans be established and maintained in accordance with a written plan document, follow a variety of disclosure and reporting requirements, and include certain minimum plan requirements. *See also* **welfare benefit plan**.

employees' profit sharing plan (EPSP). In Canada, an employer-sponsored nonregistered retirement savings plan to which the employer and employees contribute.

employee stock ownership plan (ESOP). A type of incentive compensation plan under which a company rewards individual or group performance by either allowing employees to purchase company stock or distributing company stock to employees.

employer-employee group. A type of group that generally is eligible for group insurance and that consists of the employees of a particular employer or the employees in any designated class of employees.

employment standards legislation. In Canada, legislation that mandates certain employment standards relating to such issues as minimum wage rates, overtime pay, and maximum hours of work.

endorsement. *See* **policy rider.**

endorsement method. (1) A method of transferring ownership of a life insurance policy under which the ownership change becomes effective once the policyowner notifies the insurer, in writing, of the change and the insurer records the change in its records. (2) A rarely used method of changing a life insurance policy beneficiary designation which requires the name of the new beneficiary to be added to the policy in order for the change to be effective. *Contrast with* **recording method.**

endowment insurance. Life insurance that provides a policy benefit payable either when the insured dies or on a stated date if the insured is still alive on that date.

enrollment. In group insurance, the procedures by which an eligible group member signs up for insurance coverage. In employer-employee groups, for example, new employees generally may enroll for group insurance when they are hired.

enrollment application. *See* **enrollment card.**

enrollment card. In group insurance, a form completed by each employee eligible for a group insurance plan that provides the employee's personal data, and includes a statement that the employee signs to indicate that she understands the coverage offered and agrees to have her portion of the premium deducted from her salary. Also known as *enrollment application.*

enrollment period. *See* **eligibility period.**

entire contract provision. A provision included in life insurance, health insurance, and annuity policies that defines which documents constitute the contract between the insurer and the policyowner. A typical provision might specify that the entire contract consists of the policy itself, the application if it is attached to the contract, and any attached riders.

entity accounting concept. An accounting principle stating that a company must account separately for the business activities of each basic business or economic unit.

entity method. A method of carrying out a partnership buy-sell agreement under which the partnership agrees to purchase the share of any partner who dies and to distribute a proportionate share of that ownership interest to each of the surviving partners. *Contrast with* **cross-purchase method.**

EOB. *See* **explanation of benefits.**

EPSP. *See* **employees' profit sharing plan.**

Equal Credit Opportunity Act. A U.S. federal consumer protection law that prohibits discrimination in the granting of credit on the basis of race, color, religion, national origin, sex, marital status, age, or receipt of public assistance. Creditors must provide applicants for credit, upon request, with the reasons for the denial of credit.

equity assets. Assets that represent an investor's ownership or share of ownership in an asset such as a business or property.

equity-indexed annuity. A type of annuity that offers the same type of minimum interest rate guarantees as a traditional fixed annuity, but also may credit additional interest depending upon the performance of an external standard, typically the stock market.

ERISA. *See* **Employee Retirement Income Security Act.**

errors and omissions (E&O) insurance. Insurance that protects a sales agent against financial liability for any negligent acts or mistakes.

escape clause. *See* **bailout provision.**

escrow account. A trust account used to pay property maintenance expenses, property taxes, and other expenses related to a mortgaged property.

ESOP. *See* **employee stock ownership plan.**

estate planning. A type of planning to help a client conserve, as much as possible, the personal assets that the individual wants to pass on to her heirs at her death.

ETS. *See* **Examination Tracking System.**

evergreening. A term that annuity insurers use to describe the annual delivery of an updated prospectus to variable annuity contract owners.

evidence of insurability. The proof that an insurance underwriter requires during the underwriting process in order to determine that a proposed applicant meets the insurer's health and lifestyle requirements and is an insurable risk.

evidence of insurability provision. A provision in group life and health insurance policies specifying the conditions, if any, under which the insurer reserves the right to require a person eligible for insurance to furnish evidence of insurability as a condition to all or part of her coverage.

examination report. For on-site National Association of Insurance Commissioners (NAIC) regulatory examinations in the United States, a document that summarizes the examination results and notes any adverse conditions or significant changes in an insurer's operations or financial condition. This report is submitted to both state regulators and the insurer's officers. *See also* **financial condition examination, market conduct examination,** and **on-site regulatory examination.**

Examination Tracking System (ETS). An electronic system developed by the National Association of Insurance Commissioners (NAIC) that enables the states to schedule and coordinate market conduct examinations, as well as financial examinations.

examiner. In the United States, a representative of a state insurance department who participates in market conduct and/or financial condition examinations by visiting insurers' home offices or regional offices and reviewing the insurers' business records.

examining physician. A physician who performs an examination of a proposed insured at the request of an insurance company to provide information for the underwriting process. *Contrast with* **attending physician.**

exception. *See* **exclusion.**

excess-of-loss reinsurance. A type of nonproportional reinsurance in which a reinsurer is responsible for paying the amount of a claim above a predetermined limit.

excess of retention arrangement. A method of ceding proportional reinsurance in which the ceding company establishes a dollar-amount retention limit, and the reinsurer agrees to assume amounts over the insurer's retention limit, up to the reinsurer's automatic binding limit. *See also* **automatic binding limit** and **retention limit.**

excess quota share arrangement. A method of ceding proportional reinsurance in which the ceding company keeps its full retention limit and cedes the remaining risk to two or more assuming companies on a percentage basis. *See also* **retention limit.**

exclusion. An insurance policy provision that describes circumstances under which the insurer will not pay policy benefits that otherwise would be payable. For example, self-inflicted injuries are often excluded from coverage under health insurance policies. *See also* **limitation.**

exclusionary period. For purposes of the Health Insurance Portability and Accountability Act (HIPAA) in the United States, a specified maximum period following the date an individual enrolls in a group health plan during which a preexisting condition may be excluded from coverage.

exclusion ratio. For annuities, a formula used to calculate the portion of annuity benefit payments that are excluded from the recipient's taxable income; calculated by dividing the total amount invested in the contract by the total amount expected to be returned from the contract.

exclusion rider. An amendment to an insurance policy that limits the policy's benefits by excluding from coverage certain types of risk. For example, an aviation exclusion rider might exclude from coverage a death resulting from an aviation accident.

exclusive agent. *See* **captive agent.**

exculpatory statutes. In the United States, state laws that permit an insurer to pay life insurance proceeds according to the terms of a policy without fear of double liability. Also known as *exoneration statutes.*

ex-dividend date. The date that determines whether a stockholder is eligible to receive a declared cash dividend.

exhibits. *See* **schedules.**

exoneration statutes. *See* **exculpatory statutes.**

expected claim experience. For a particular group insurance plan, the dollar amount of claims that the insurer estimates the group will submit.

expected mortality. The number or rate of deaths that have been predicted to occur in a group of people at a given age according to a mortality table. Also known as *tabular mortality. Contrast with* **mortality experience.**

expense. An amount of assets a company either (1) spends to obtain a benefit or service or (2) allocates to provide for required reserves. Also known as *cost. See also* **operating expenses.**

expense budget. A schedule of expenses expected during an accounting period.

expense charge. When pricing insurance products, the portion of the product's pricing structure that is designed to reimburse the insurer for its operating expenses—specifically commissions, premium taxes, and general operating expenses.

expense margin. When pricing insurance products, the difference between the amount needed to cover expenses and the expense level the insurer uses to price a product.

expense participation feature. *See* **coinsurance.**

experience rating. A method of calculating group insurance premium rates by which the insurer considers the particular group's prior claims and expense experience. *See also* **manual rating** and **pooling.**

experience refund. For a particular group insurance plan, the portion of a group insurance premium that is returned to a group policyholder whose claim experience is better than had been anticipated when the premium was calculated. Also known as *dividend.*

explanation of benefits (EOB). A detailed statement sent to an insured that shows each treatment or medication submitted as part of a health insurance claim, an insurer's decision concerning payment of each charge, any amount that is considered as a deductible or a copayment, an explanation of any charge for which part or all of the charge will not be paid, and the total amount sent to a health care provider.

extended congregate care facility (ECCF). For purposes of long-term care insurance, a type of assisted living facility that offers more extensive custodial care than an adult congregate living facility, but less than that of a nursing home. *See also* **adult congregate living facility** and **nursing home.**

extended spouse's allowance. In Canada, the Old Age Security (OAS) benefit payable to a person who has been receiving a spouse's allowance and whose spouse dies. The benefit is payable until the recipient reaches age 65 or remarries. *See also* **Old Age Security (OAS) Act.**

extended term insurance option. One of several nonforfeiture options included in life insurance policies that allows the owner of a policy with a cash value to discontinue premium payments and to use the policy's net cash value to purchase term insurance for the full coverage amount provided under the original policy for as long a term as the net cash value can provide. *See also* **nonforfeiture options.**

extended-time reinsurance. A type of nonproportional reinsurance in which the reinsurer takes over paying benefits after the ceding company has paid benefits for a certain amount of time.

external audit. An examination and evaluation of any company's records and procedures conducted by an accounting firm not associated with the organization. Also known as *independent audit. Contrast with* **internal audit.** (1) For an insurance company, an external audit includes an evaluation of the company's financial statements; the issuance of an opinion as to whether those financial statements present fairly the company's operations through adherence to GAAP, statutory accounting, or other accounting principles; and a recommendation of changes to the company's system of internal control. (2) In reinsurance, an external audit includes an on-site inspection of the procedures, controls, and records of a party to a reinsurance treaty. Also known as *due-diligence review.*

external customer. Any person or business who has purchased or is using a company's products or is in a position to buy or use the company's products. *Contrast with* **internal customer.**

external replacement. *See* **replacement.**

extra-contract damages. In a lawsuit brought against an insurance company, money awards to the plaintiff that exceed the amount of the insurance policy benefits and which are compensatory or punitive in nature. *See also* **compensatory damages** and **punitive damages.**

extra-percentage table. A method insurers use to develop premium charges for substandard risks, wherein each substandard class is charged a higher than usual premium rate that reflects a multiple of the insurer's mortality rates for standard risks.

face amount. For a fixed-amount whole life insurance policy, the amount of the death benefit payable if the insured person dies while the policy is in force.

face-to-face assessment. In long-term care (LTC) insurance underwriting, a meeting between a proposed insured and an interviewer who represents the insurance company and who is usually employed by a vendor to observe an applicant's physical and mental condition. *Contrast with* **functional assessment.**

face value. For a bond or other debt security, the amount stated on the security.

facility-of-payment clause. A life insurance policy provision that permits the insurance company to pay all or part of the policy proceeds either to a relative of the insured or to anyone who has a valid claim to those proceeds.

fac-ob. *See* **facultative-obligatory reinsurance.**

factor table. A chart insurers use to prescribe the amount of life or disability income insurance coverage which an insurance applicant is eligible to purchase. This chart shows the maximum amount of insurance, expressed in multiples of a person's salary or total income, that an insurer will typically approve in each of several age ranges. *See also* **percentage of income rule.**

facultative-obligatory (fac-ob) reinsurance. A type of reinsurance agreement that allows a ceding company to choose whether to submit cases to a reinsurer and requires the reinsurer to accept the cases based on the ceding company's underwriting, up to an amount defined in the agreement, if the reinsurer has available capacity. *Contrast with* **automatic reinsurance.**

facultative reinsurance. A type of reinsurance agreement that allows (1) a ceding company to choose whether to ask a reinsurer to consider coverage on a risk, (2) the reinsurer to choose whether it wishes to participate in the risk, and (3) the ceding company to choose whether to accept the reinsurer's offer on the risk, if an offer is made. *Contrast with* **automatic reinsurance.**

Fair Credit Reporting Act (FCRA). In the United States, a federal law that regulates the reporting and use of consumer credit information and seeks to ensure that reports from consumer reporting agencies contain only accurate, relevant, and recent information. *See also* **consumer credit report** and **consumer reporting agency.**

Fair Labor Standards Act (FLSA). In the United States, a federal law that establishes minimum wage, overtime pay, record keeping, and child labor standards that affect workers in most private companies and federal, state, and local governments.

fair market value. *See* **current market value.**

Family and Medical Leave Act (FMLA). Federal legislation in the United States that requires companies with 50 or more employees within a 75-mile radius to grant eligible employees an unpaid leave of up to 12 weeks for family and medical emergencies, including childbirth, adoption, and illness of a child, spouse, parent, or the employee.

family benefit coverage. A type of supplementary benefit rider offered in conjunction with a life insurance policy that insures the lives of the insured's spouse and children. Also known as *dependent life insurance* and *spouse and children's insurance rider.*

family income coverage. A plan of decreasing term life insurance that provides a stated monthly income benefit amount to the insured's surviving spouse if the insured dies during the term of coverage. The benefit amount provides an income for a predetermined period to help support the insured's family.

family policy. A type of life insurance policy that covers all the members of a family under one contract. The primary insured is issued a whole life insurance policy; and the insured's spouse and children receive term life insurance coverage.

FASB. *See* **Financial Accounting Standards Board.**

FAST system. *See* **Financial Analysis and Solvency Tracking System.**

favorable deviation. In insurance product design, a difference between actual and assumed product values that produces an increase in actual product profitability relative to assumed product profitability. *Contrast with* **adverse deviation.**

favorable variance. In accounting, a cost variance in which the standard cost is higher than the actual cost. *Contrast with* **unfavorable variance.**

FCRA. *See* **Fair Credit Reporting Act.**

FDIC. *See* **Federal Deposit Insurance Corporation.**

Fed. *See* **Federal Reserve System.**

Federal Deposit Insurance Corporation (FDIC). In the United States, a federal agency that insures deposits made into member banks and savings and loans up to $100,000 per person/per institution.

Federal Reserve System. In the United States, the federal banking system that is made up of 12 regional banks and member state and national banks and is designed, among other things, to supervise and regulate member banks and protect the credit rights of consumers. Often referred to as *the Fed.*

Federal Trade Commission (FTC). A U.S. federal regulatory agency that enforces antitrust and trade practices laws. The FTC is empowered to, among other things, (1) prevent unfair methods of competition, and unfair or deceptive acts or practices in or affecting commerce; (2) seek monetary redress and other relief for conduct that injures consumers; (3) adopt trade regulation rules to define specific acts or practices that are unfair or deceptive and establish requirements designed to prevent such acts or practices; (4) conduct investigations relating to the organization, business, practices, and management of entities engaged in commerce; and (5) make reports and legislative recommendations to Congress.

Federal Unemployment Tax Act. Federal legislation in the United States that, when combined with individual state laws, provides covered individuals with protection against loss of income resulting from unemployment.

fee schedule payment structure. A payment method some health maintenance organizations (HMOs) use to reimburse medical care providers that places maximum limits on the dollar amounts the HMO will pay for covered medical procedures and services.

Fellow of the Society of Actuaries (FSA). A professional designation that an actuary may use when he or she completes a course of examination in addition to those completed for the ASA. *See also* **Associate of the Society of Actuaries (ASA).**

fiduciary. A person or other legal entity who holds a special position of trust or confidence when handling the business affairs of another and who must put the other's interests above his or her own.

field advisory councils. Groups of insurance sales agents who provide feedback about a new insurance product.

field force. An insurer's collective sales agents.

field office. An insurance company's local sales office. Also known as *insurance agency.*

field officer. A home service insurance marketing officer who supervises district managers and carries out large-scale marketing planning. Also known as *regional vice president.*

field underwriting manual. A document, developed by an insurance company, that presents specific guidance for an agent's assessment of the risk represented by a proposed insured, and guides the agent in assembling and submitting the evidence of insurability needed for the underwriter to evaluate the risk.

fifth dividend option. *See* **additional term insurance option.**

file and use requirement. In the United States, a regulatory policy under which an insurer may use certain policy forms after filing those forms with the state insurance department.

financial accounting. A field of accounting that focuses primarily on reporting a company's financial information to meet the needs of the company's external users.

Financial Accounting Standards Board (FASB). A private organization, funded by the accounting profession and companies with an interest in accounting practices, that establishes and promotes the use of generally accepted accounting principles (GAAP) in the United States.

Financial Analysis and Solvency Tracking (FAST) system. A system used by the National Association of Insurance Commissioners (NAIC) in the United States to detect financial distress in large insurance companies. The FAST system uses two types of analysis to examine an insurer's financial statement information: ratio analysis of the insurer's most recent financial statements, and analysis of the five-year history of specific aspects of the insurer's financial statements.

financial auditing. The process of examining and evaluating company records and procedures to ensure that the company's accounting records and financial statements are presented fairly and reasonably, quality assurance is maintained, and operational procedures and policies are effective.

financial condition examination. In the United States, a type of routine on-site regulatory investigation of insurers for the purpose of identifying and monitoring any threats to the insurer's solvency *Contrast with* **market conduct examination.** *See also* **on-site regulatory examination.**

Financial Disclosure Form. A form that some insurers require an insurance applicant to read, understand, and sign, which provides information about an insurance product's investment options, expenses, charges, and other specifics.

financial institution. A business entity that collects funds from net suppliers of funds and places these funds in financial assets, thus channeling the funds to net users of funds. Also known as *financial intermediary.*

financial intermediary. *See* **financial institution.**

financial instrument. *See* **security.**

financial leverage. The magnification of an entity's risk and return that occurs when the entity incurs fixed financing costs, usually by borrowing funds.

financial planner. A professional who analyzes a client's financial circumstances and goals and prepares a program, usually in writing, to meet the client's financial goals.

financial planning. A coordinated process for identifying, planning for, and meeting goals related to financial needs for individuals, families, and small businesses.

financial ratio. A percentage that expresses a relationship between two pieces of financial information.

financial ratio analysis. The process of calculating the relationships between various pairs of financial statement values for the purpose of assessing a company's financial condition or performance.

financial reinsurance. Reinsurance coverage that allows a ceding insurance company to improve its financial position through the timing and the method of risk transfer. *See also* **ceding company** and **reinsurance.**

financial reporting. The process of presenting financial data about a company's financial position, the company's operating performance, and its flow of funds for an accounting period.

financial risk. The risk that a business will be unable to pay its financial obligations on time.

financial services industry. Financial institutions that help consumers, businesses, and governments save, borrow, invest, and otherwise manage money. *See also* financial institution.

Financial Services Modernization Act. *See* **Gramm-Leach-Bliley (GLB) Act.**

financial statements. Standardized reports of a company's major monetary events and transactions.

financial subsidiary. According to the Gramm-Leach-Bliley Act in the United States, a corporation that is owned or controlled by a financial holding company and engages in specified financial activities.

financial transaction. A business transaction to which a company must assign an objective monetary value, whether the impact on the company is large or small, actual or expected.

financial worksheet. A document used during the underwriting of insurance that enables an underwriter to organize an insurance applicant's financial information and to develop a clear picture of the person's financial situation.

financing activities. Transactions that involve borrowed funds and cash payments to or from a company's owners.

fire policy. A homeowner insurance policy that covers the insured dwelling and/or contents from damage caused by fire and other perils, such as smoke, riot, hail, tornado, explosion, and lightning.

first-dollar coverage. Medical expense insurance coverage under which the insurer begins to reimburse the insured for the payment of eligible medical expenses without first requiring the insured to satisfy a deductible or coinsurance amount.

first dollar quota share arrangement. A method of proportional reinsurance in which a ceding company cedes a certain percentage of the entire risk to an assuming company or companies despite the presence of a retention limit—that is, the ceding company cedes coverage from the first dollar. *See also* **ceding company, reinsurance,** and **retention limit.**

first excess. In a layering reinsurance arrangement involving two or more reinsurers, the amount in excess of an insurer's retention limit up to a specified amount. *See also* **layering** and **second excess.**

first-to-die life insurance. *See* **joint life insurance.**

fiscal year. A 12-month accounting period chosen by a company for financial reporting purposes.

fixed account. For a variable annuity, an investment subaccount into which contract owners can place money that will earn a guaranteed fixed rate of interest for a specified period of time. Also known as *variable guaranteed account. See also* **subaccount.**

fixed account provision. A variable life insurance policy provision that defines a fixed account and stipulates the minimum annual interest rate for the account. Also known as *general account provision.*

fixed-amount budget. *See* **static budget.**

fixed amount option. (1) A life insurance policy settlement option under which the insurer pays equal installments of a stated amount until the policy proceeds, plus the interest earned, are exhausted. *See also* **settlement options.** (2) An annuity payout option under which the insurer determines the length of time that the annuity's accumulated value will provide a pre-selected periodic payment. *See also* **payout options.**

fixed annuity. An annuity for which the insurer assumes the contract's investment risk and guarantees to pay a specified rate of interest on the accumulated value for a specified period of time. Premiums paid for a fixed annuity are paid into an insurer's general account. *Contrast with* **variable annuity.** *See also* **deferred annuity** and **immediate annuity.**

fixed budget. *See* **static budget.**

fixed cost. A business cost that remains constant regardless of the level of operating activity or production. *Contrast with* **variable cost.**

fixed dividends. Preferred stock dividend payments that are fixed in both schedule and amount.

fixed payout. A type of annuity payment guaranteed to remain the same throughout the payout period. *See also* **payout period.**

fixed period option. (1) A life insurance policy settlement option under which the insurer pays the policy proceeds and interest in a series of annual or more frequent installments for a preselected period. *See also* **settlement options**. (2) An annuity payout option under which the insurer makes annuity payments for a specified period of time. *See also* **payout options**.

flat extra premium method. In life insurance, an approach to calculating the premium amount for substandard risks when the extra risk is considered to be constant. For every $1,000 of insurance applied-for, a specified extra dollar amount will be added to the standard premium. Also known as *flat rating*.

flat rating. *See* **flat extra premium method.**

flexible-amount budget. *See* **flexible budget.**

flexible benefits plan. An employee benefit plan in which each employee receives a statement of the total dollar amount of optional benefits available to him; each employee then decides which benefits he wants and allocates his funds to pay for those benefits. Also known as *cafeteria plan*.

flexible budget. A budget that provides alternative sets of budget estimates to use under the different circumstances that may arise during an accounting period. Also known as *dynamic budget* and *variable budget.*

flexible premium. A premium payment method sometimes offered in connection with annuities and with some types of life insurance that allows the contract owner or policyowner to alter the amount and the frequency of payments, within specified boundaries defined by the insurer and the law.

FLSA. *See* **Fair Labor Standards Act.**

FMLA. *See* **Family and Medical Leave Act.**

foreclosure. A legal procedure by which a lender recovers an unpaid loan balance by obtaining title to the real property offered as collateral if the borrower fails to make timely contractual principal and interest payments on the loan.

foreign corporation. (1) From the point of view of any state in the United States, an insurance company that is incorporated under the laws of another state. (2) In Canada, a company that is incorporated under the laws of another country. Also known as *nonresident corporation.*

Foreign Insurance Companies Act. A Canadian federal statute which describes the requirements that foreign insurers must meet in order to transact business in Canada. *See also* **foreign corporation.**

forfeiture. Any pension plan account balance abandoned by participants who leave the plan before they have a right to keep those benefits.

Form 1099. *See* **IRS Form 1099.**

Form 5498. *See* **IRS Form 5498.**

formal contract. A contract that is enforceable because the parties to the contract met certain formalities concerning the form of the agreement. For example, formal contracts generally must be in writing and must contain some form of seal in order to be enforceable. *Contrast with* **informal contract.**

forward contracts. Limited time agreements in which a seller promises to deliver a specified investment to a buyer sometime in the future for a price that is specified in the agreement. *See also* **futures contracts.**

forward pricing rules. In the United States, Security and Exchange Commission (SEC) rules that govern the subaccount values that insurers must use to process contributions to and distributions from variable annuities.

fraternal benefit society. *See* **fraternal insurer.**

fraternal insurer. A nonprofit organization that is operated solely for the benefit of its members and that provides its members with social and insurance benefits. Also known as *fraternal benefit society.*

fraud. An act by which someone intentionally deceives another party and induces that other party to part with something of value.

fraudulent claim. An insurance claim for which the claimant attempts to collect policy benefits by providing false information to an insurer.

free-examination provision. *See* **free-look provision.**

free-look provision. A life insurance, health insurance, and annuity policy provision that allows the policyowner or contract owner a specified period, usually at least 10 days, following policy delivery within which to cancel the policy and receive a refund of all premiums paid. Also known as *ten-day free look provision.*

free surplus. *See* **divisible surplus.**

free withdrawal provision. Deferred annuity contract provision which gives the contract owner the right to withdraw a portion of the accumulated value without paying a surrender charge and defines how the free withdrawal amount will be determined.

front-end load. A sales charge that a purchaser of an investment product pays at the time of the purchase to defray the sales commission which a sales producer collected for selling the product. Also known as *sales charge. Contrast with* **back-end load.** *See also* **no-load fund.**

fronting. A reinsurance arrangement in which a licensed insurer, known as the *fronting company*, issues a policy on a risk for, and at the request of, one or more other unlicensed insurers with the intent of ceding the entire risk to the other insurer or insurers through reinsurance.

front-load annuity. *See* **front-loaded policy.**

front-loaded policy. A life insurance policy or a deferred annuity contract in which most of the expense charges associated with acquiring the business are included in the premium payments for the product. *Contrast with* **back-loaded policy.**

FSA. *See* **Fellow of the Society of Actuaries.**

FTC. *See* **Federal Trade Commission.**

fulfillment kit. When selling insurance through a direct response distribution system, the package of materials designed to address or "fulfill" a respondent's request for insurance.

full-disclosure accounting concept. An accounting principle which states that a company's financial statements must contain all material information about the company and that the company must disclose any additional information or fact that, by its omission, could mislead an interested user of the company's financial information.

full portability provision. A group long-term care (LTC) policy provision that allows a person to continue coverage under the group LTC policy after leaving the group.

full-scope regulatory examination. In the United States, a state regulatory examination of an insurer's financial position taken as a whole to identify insurers having financial difficulties. *Contrast with* **limited-scope regulatory examination.**

fully-insured group plan. A group insurance plan for which the group policyholder makes monthly premium payments to the insurance company and the insurer is financially responsible for paying all claim payments or benefit payments to the group insureds. *Contrast with* **self-insured group plan.**

fully-insured pension plan. A pension plan for which an insurance company is financially responsible for the payment of pension benefits. Pension benefits may be provided for plan participants through group contracts covering a group of participants or individual contracts for each participant. *See also* **deposit administration contract, group deferred annuity,** and **immediate participation guarantee (IPG) contract.**

functional assessment. In long-term care (LTC) insurance underwriting, the process of examining the cognitive status of the proposed insured and the extent to which the proposed insured is able to perform the activities of daily living. *Contrast with* **face-to-face assessment.** *See also* **activities of daily living** and **cognitive impairment.**

functional cost analysis. An accounting cost control tool in which the accumulated costs for a functional activity within an organization are compiled and compared with previous data or with comparable data from similar organizations.

functional costs. The accumulated costs of the activities involved within a certain function, without regard to organizational units.

funding vehicle. The means for investing the assets of a retirement plan as those assets are accumulated. The two primary funding vehicles for pension plans are trusteed pension plans and fully-insured pension plans. *See also* **combination pension plan, fully-insured pension plan,** and **trusteed pension plan.**

future purchase option benefit. A supplemental benefit that is provided by some disability income policies and that gives the insured the right to increase the policy's benefit amount in accordance with increases in the insured's earnings usually without providing evidence of insurability.

future value (FV). The value of a sum of money—invested at a specified interest rate—at the end of a given period of time. *Contrast with* **present value (PV).**

future value interest factor (FVIF). A number used to calculate at a specified interest rate the future value of a present amount as of a given time. A *future value interest factors table* shows the future value of $1.00 for various interest rates and a number of compounding periods. *Contrast with* **present value interest factor (PVIF).**

future value interest factor for an annuity (FVIFA). A number that represents the future value of a $1.00 annuity at a given rate of interest and for a stated number of periods. Also known as *compound value interest factor for an annuity. Contrast with* **present value interest factor for an annuity (PVIFA).**

future value of an annuity. The amount that a series of equal payments earning a given rate of compound interest will accumulate by a given future date. *Contrast with* **present value of an annuity.**

future value of an annuity due (FVAd). The future value of an annuity in which the payment occurs at the beginning of each payment period. *Contrast with* **future value of an ordinary annuity (FVA).**

future value of an ordinary annuity (FVA). The future value of an annuity in which the payment occurs at the end of each payment period. *Contrast with* **future value of an annuity due (FVAd).**

futures contracts. Limited-time agreements that give the owner of the agreement the right to buy or sell a specified investment in the future for a price that is set through trading on an organized exchange. *See also* **forward contracts.**

FV. *See* **future value.**

FVA. *See* **future value of an ordinary annuity.**

FVAd. *See* **future value of an annuity due.**

FVIF. *See* **future value interest factor.**

FVIFA. *See* **future value interest factor for an annuity.**

GA. *See* **general agent.**

GAAP. *See* **generally accepted accounting principles.**

GAAP accounting records. Accounting records, designed for financial reporting to investors and the public at large, that focus on showing the company's financial stability along with its profitability. GAAP accounting records are prepared according to generally accepted accounting principles. *Contrast with* **statutory accounting records.**

gatekeeper. A term used to describe the primary care physician's role in a managed health care plan; this role is to authorize all medical services delivered to the insured by other physicians or health care providers.

gender-based mortality table. *See* **sex-distinct mortality table.**

general account. An undivided investment account in which insurers maintain funds that support contractual obligations for guaranteed insurance products such as whole life insurance or fixed-rate annuities. *Contrast with* **separate account.**

general agency system. A type of ordinary agency insurance distribution system wherein general agents establish and maintain field sales offices for an insurance company. *See also* **general agent** and **ordinary agency distribution system.**

general agent (GA). An independent businessperson who is under contract to an insurance company and whose primary function is to build and manage a field office of full-time career agents focused on distributing the products of a single company within a defined territory. *See also* **general agency system.**

general and administrative expenses. For an insurance company, the costs incurred as a result of an insurer's normal business operations, including both contractual benefit expenses and operating expenses.

generally accepted accounting principles (GAAP). A set of financial accounting standards that all publicly traded companies in the United States and all companies in Canada follow when preparing their financial statements. *Contrast with* **statutory accounting practices.**

general management risk. *See* C-4 risk.

general manager. *See* branch manager.

GI benefit. *See* guaranteed insurability benefit.

GIC. *See* guaranteed investment contract.

GIS. *See* Guaranteed Income Supplement.

GLB Act. *See* Gramm-Leach-Bliley Act.

going-concern concept. An accounting principle that requires a company's accounting records to reflect the assumption that the company will continue to operate indefinitely.

government bonds. Bonds issued by governments—including federal, state, provincial, county, city, and local governments. *See also* bonds.

grace period. (1) For insurance premium payments, a specified length of time following a premium due date within which the renewal premium may be paid without penalty. The length of the grace period is specified in a *grace period provision* that is found in a life insurance, health insurance, or annuity policy. (2) For purchases made on credit, a period of time between the date of a purchase and the date the lender begins to charge interest during which no interest accrues.

graded-premium policy. A type of modified-premium whole life policy that calls for three or more levels of annual premium payment amounts, increasing at specified points in time—such as every three years—until reaching the amount to be paid as a level premium for the rest of the life of the policy.

Gramm-Leach-Bliley (GLB) Act. An act passed by the U.S. Congress in 1999, which allows convergence among the traditionally separate components of the financial services industry—banks, securities firms, and insurance companies. The GLB Act permits financial institutions to affiliate in new ways and expands the ability of national banks to market insurance products. Also known as *Financial Services Modernization Act.*

gross annuity cost. A monetary amount equal to the present value of future periodic income payments under an annuity contract, calculated on a gross basis, with a specific provision for expense loading. *Contrast with* net annuity cost.

gross debt. For purposes of determining the benefit payable under a consumer credit insurance policy, the total of the remaining scheduled payments on a given date.

gross estate. The total value of all property in which a deceased person—known as the *decedent*—had an ownership interest.

gross investment income. Total investment income actually earned, on an accrual-basis and before deducting expenses and amortization, during a specified reporting period.

gross leverage ratio. *See* **insurance leverage ratio.**

gross premium. The amount of money an insurer actually charges for an insurance policy. The gross premium is equal to the policy's net premium plus the loading. *Contrast with* **net premium.** *See also* **loading.**

gross reserve. A reserve developed using a gross reserve valuation method.

gross reserve valuation method. A method of computing reserves which makes explicit provision for product-related expenses or loading.

group annuity. A retirement plan funding arrangement that provides periodic income payments at retirement to a group of people under a single group contract. *See also* **group deferred annuity, deposit administration contract,** and **immediate participation guarantee (IPG) contract.**

group creditor life insurance. Insurance issued to a creditor, such as a bank, to insure the lives of the creditor's current and future debtors.

group deferred annuity. A retirement plan funding vehicle under which contributions made on behalf of each plan participant in a group are used to purchase a series of single-premium deferred annuities for the participant. When the participant retires, the deferred annuities provide the promised benefits. *Contrast with* **immediate participation guarantee (IPG) contract.**

Group Health Insurance Definition and Group Health Insurance Standard Provisions Model Act. A National Association of Insurance Commissioners (NAIC) model law that defines the types of groups eligible for group health insurance and specifies standard provisions that group health insurance policies must include.

Group Health Insurance Mandatory Conversion Privilege Model Act. A National Association of Insurance Commissioners (NAIC) model law that requires specified types of group health insurance policies to give insureds the right to obtain individual health insurance without providing evidence of insurability in specified situations.

group insurance. A method of providing life or health insurance coverage for a group of people under one insurance contract, called a *master contract*. *See also* **master contract** and **policyholder.**

group insured. An individual insured by a group insurance policy.

Group Life Insurance Definition and Group Life Insurance Standard Provisions Model Act. A National Association of Insurance Commissioners (NAIC) model law that defines the types of groups that are eligible for group life insurance and specifies standard provisions that group life insurance policies must include.

group plan installation. In group insurance, all the activities that occur from the time a prospective buyer decides to purchase a group insurance policy to the time the coverage is fully explained to the group members and the master contract and its individual certificates are issued. *See also* **master contract** and **certificate of insurance.**

group policyholder. *See* **policyholder.**

group representative. A salaried insurance company employee who is trained to market and service group insurance products.

guaranteed death benefit. In a variable universal life insurance policy, a minimum death benefit amount that will be provided regardless of the underlying policy's cash value at the time of the death of the insured.

guaranteed income contract. *See* **guaranteed investment contract (GIC).**

Guaranteed Income Supplement (GIS). In Canada, a government-provided supplemental monthly benefit available to Old Age Security (OAS) recipients who receive less income than a stated maximum amount.

guaranteed insurability (GI) benefit. A supplementary life insurance policy benefit often provided through a policy rider that gives the policyowner the right to purchase additional insurance of the same type as the life insurance policy that provides the GI benefit on specified option dates. Also known as *guaranteed insurability option (GIO).*

guaranteed interest contract. *See* **guaranteed investment contract (GIC).**

guaranteed investment contract (GIC). A retirement plan funding vehicle under which an insurer accepts a single deposit from the group plan sponsor for a specified period. The insurer invests the funds, and guarantees the plan sponsor at least a specified investment return. Also known as *guaranteed interest contract* and *guaranteed income contract.*

guaranteed-issue insurance product. An insurance product designed so that every eligible member of a particular group of proposed insureds who applies for and meets specified conditions is automatically issued a policy, and no individual underwriting takes place.

guaranteed maximum mortality rate. In a universal life (UL) insurance policy, an upper limit on the monthly mortality charge an insurer is permitted to apply to the policy. *See also* **mortality rate.**

guaranteed minimum payout annuity. A type of annuity contract that promises to pay a specified minimum dollar amount or a specified minimum number of payments. The minimum payout can take the form of a lump sum or installments.

guaranteed purchase option. A policy provision sometimes included in long-term care (LTC) insurance policies that allows an insured person to increase the original daily benefit amount at intervals specified in the policy without having to provide evidence of insurability.

guaranteed renewable policy. An individual health insurance policy that requires the insurer to renew the policy—as long as premium payments are made—at least until the insured attains a specified age. The insurer can change premium rates for broad classes of insureds but not for an individual insured. *Contrast with* **noncancellable and guaranteed renewable policy.**

guaranty association. In the United States, an organization that is composed of all the life insurance companies operating in a state and that is responsible for covering the financial obligations of member companies that become insolvent.

guaranty association disclaimer. In the United States, a document that notifies the purchaser of an insurance or annuity contract of the existence of the state life and health guaranty association and that, in the event of the insurer's insolvency, the purchaser may not be totally protected by the guaranty association.

guaranty-fund assessment. A charge payable by financially-sound insurers that are members of a state guaranty association as a contribution toward the customer obligations of a failed member insurer.

Guidelines Governing Group Accident and Sickness Insurance. In Canada, Superintendent's Guidelines that regulate several aspects of group health insurance contracts, including the types of groups to which a group health insurance contract may be issued and the particulars that must be included in the certificate issued to each person insured by the contract.

Guide to Buying Life Insurance. A written statement developed by the Canadian Life and Health Insurance Association (CLHIA) that describes all of the types of life insurance available, so that a prospect for life insurance can compare the advantages and disadvantages of each type of policy. *See also* **Buyer's Guide.**

hands-on assistance. For long-term care (LTC) insurance, the actual physical assistance provided to a person who is in the course of performing activities of daily living. *See also* **activities of daily living** and **substantial assistance.**

HCFA. *See* **Health Care Financing Administration.**

head office. *See* **home office.**

Health Care Financing Administration (HCFA). In the United States, the division of the federal Department of Health and Human Services responsible for administering the Medicare and Medicaid programs. *See also* **Medicaid** and **Medicare.**

health insurance. A type of insurance coverage that provides benefits for an insured's sickness, injury, or disability. *See also* **disability income insurance, long-term care (LTC) insurance,** and **medical expense insurance.**

Health Insurance Portability and Accountability Act (HIPAA). A U.S. federal law that imposes a number of requirements on group and individual health insurance plans, health insurers, and health maintenance organizations (HMOs) and that is designed to improve the availability and portability of health insurance benefits. HIPAA establishes federal standards for the continuation of health care benefits for people who change jobs, are self-employed, or who have preexisting medical conditions.

health maintenance organization (HMO). A health care plan that combines the financing and delivery of health care to provide comprehensive health care services for subscribing members in a particular geographic area in exchange for a prepaid fee.

Health Maintenance Organizations (HMOs) Model Act. A National Association of Insurance Commissioners (NAIC) model law that regulates all aspects of the organization and operation of HMOs conducting business in a state that has enacted such a law.

heaped commission system. An insurance sales commission system that features relatively high first-year commissions and lower renewal commissions.

hedging. An investment strategy that combines different types of securities in a given investment portfolio in order to reduce the overall riskiness of the portfolio's asset mix.

high water mark method. A method for crediting excess interest to an equity-indexed annuity that involves comparing the value of the index at the beginning of the term of the contract with the highest value that the index reaches at certain points, usually contract anniversary dates, during the term.

HIPAA. *See* **Health Insurance Portability and Accountability Act.**

historical cost. In accounting and investing, the original purchase price of an asset.

history statement. In the underwriting of insurance, a statement from an attending physician concerning a specific health condition that a proposed insured has admitted as having on the insurance application.

HMO. *See* **health maintenance organization.**

home health care. For long-term care (LTC) insurance, skilled or nonskilled nursing care, physical therapy, and home health assistance provided by a state-licensed and/or Medicare-certified home health agency.

home office. An insurance company's headquarters, where most of the functional areas—such as underwriting, claim administration, customer service, actuarial, marketing, accounting, legal/compliance, and human resources—are located. *See also* **regional office.**

homeowner's insurance. A type of insurance that protects an insured from the financial losses resulting from damage to the insured's home or contents or resulting from being held liable for the losses of others suffered while on the insured's property.

home service agent. A commissioned insurance sales agent who sells a range of products and provides specified policyowner services, including the collection of renewal premiums, within a specified geographic area. Also known as *debit agent.*

home service distribution system. A method of selling and servicing insurance policies through commissioned sales agents who sell a range of products and provide specified policyowner services, including the collection of renewal premiums, within a specified geographic area.

horizontal analysis. A type of financial statement analysis that involves calculating the absolute amount and the percentage of the increase or decrease in a specified financial statement from one reporting period to another. *Contrast with* **vertical analysis.**

hospice. A facility that specializes in the treatment of terminally ill people, typically providing the services of doctors and nurses to care for a patient and provide pain relief 24 hours a day.

hospice benefit. A health insurance policy benefit that provides for the payment of medical or nonmedical treatments for terminally ill insureds either at the insured's home or at a designated medical facility. *See also* **hospice.**

hospital confinement indemnity coverage. A type of health insurance coverage that provides a flat benefit amount for each day an insured is hospitalized up to a predetermined number of days. The benefit does not vary according to the amount of medical expenses the insured incurs. For example, a policy might provide $20 per day for a period of at least 31 days during any hospital confinement.

HR 10 plan. *See* **Keogh plan.**

human resources. The function within a business organization that monitors the availability of qualified workers; recruits and screens applicants for jobs; helps select qualified employees; plans and presents appropriate orientation, training, and development for each employee; and administers employee benefit programs.

IADLs. *See* **instrumental activities of daily living.**

IASC. *See* **International Accounting Standards Committee.**

IBNR claims. *See* **incurred but not reported claims.**

ICD. *See* **International Classification of Diseases and Related Health Problems.**

illegal occupation provision. An individual health insurance policy provision which states that the insurer will not be liable for any loss that results from the insured's committing or attempting to commit a felony or from the insured's engaging in an illegal occupation.

illustration. As defined by the National Association of Insurance Commissioners (NAIC) Life Insurance Illustrations Model Regulation in the United States, a life insurance sales presentation or depiction that portrays nonguaranteed values of a life insurance policy, portrays these values over a period of years, and is shown to a potential customer.

illustration actuary. In the United States, an insurance company employee or a consultant hired by an insurer who meets requirements specified in the Life Insurance Illustrations Model Regulation and who is responsible for ensuring that the scales used to calculate the nonguaranteed values in the insurer's life insurance sales illustrations meet the requirements of the Model Regulation.

illustration of net cost. In a proposal for group insurance, an explanation of rates that typically covers two or more years and shows possible future ratings and premiums, provided the group's claim experience stays within the parameters assumed for the insurance product.

immediate annuity. An annuity under which periodic income benefit payments are scheduled to begin one annuity period after the contract's issue date. *Contrast with* **deferred annuity.** *See also* **annuity period.**

immediate expense recognition. In accounting, an expense recognition concept, which states that a company must recognize all costs as expenses during the current accounting period.

immediate participation guarantee (IPG) contract. A type of group annuity contract used to fund employee retirement benefits that does not guarantee a minimum investment return or provide full guarantees against investment loss. Under this type of plan, the insurer places the plan assets in an investment account in the name of the plan sponsor, and plan assets share in the gains or losses relating to the activities of investing and paying pension benefits. When a plan participant retires, the plan sponsor may withdraw funds to purchase an immediate annuity for that retiree or the monthly retirement benefit may be paid directly from the investment account to the retiree. *See also* **deposit administration contract.**

impairment. For insurance underwriting purposes, any aspect of a proposed insured's present health, medical history, health habits, family history, occupation, or other activities that could increase that person's expected mortality risk.

impairment guide. A document that insurance sales agents use when gathering information about a proposed insured that lists common impairments and the probable underwriting decision for proposed insureds who have these types of impairments. *See also* **impairment.**

impairment rider. An amendment to an insurance policy that excludes from coverage any loss that arises from a specified disease or physical impairment, or concerns a specific body part. Also known as *impairment waiver* and *exclusion rider.*

impairment waiver. *See* **impairment rider.**

IMR. *See* **interest maintenance reserve.**

IMSA. *See* **Insurance Marketplace Standards Association.**

income date. The date on which an insurer begins or is scheduled to begin making annuity benefit payments under an annuity contract. Also known as *maturity date* and *annuity date.*

income protection insurance. A type of disability income coverage that provides an income benefit both, while the insured is totally disabled and unable to work and while he is able to work, but because of a disability, is earning less than he earned before being disabled. Also known as *residual disability insurance.*

income replacement table. For disability income coverage, a table that presents the limits on the amount of disability income insurance—usually expressed as an amount of monthly benefit—an insurer will issue based on an applicant's earned income.

income statement. A financial document that provides information on a business organization's revenues and expenses during a specified period and indicates whether the business experienced a net income or net loss during the period. Also known as *statement of operations.*

income tax. A tax that is levied on income that a person or business earns.

Income Tax Act. A Canadian law that encourages the creation of private pension plans by according favorable tax treatment to plans registered with Revenue Canada.

incontestability provision. An insurance and annuity policy provision that limits the time within which an insurer has the right to avoid the contract on the ground of material misrepresentation in the application for the policy. Also known as *incontestable clause. See also* **contestable period** and **time limit on certain defenses provision.**

increasing term life insurance. A type of term life insurance that provides a death benefit that increases by some specified amount or percentage at stated intervals over the policy term. *Contrast with* **decreasing term life insurance.**

incremental cost. *See* **marginal cost.**

incurred but not reported (IBNR) claims. In the United States, insurance claims that were incurred during an accounting period but that have not been reported to the insurer as of the Annual Statement date.

indemnity benefits. Contractual benefits that are based on the actual amount of financial loss. In traditional medical expense insurance plans, insureds are reimbursed for the covered medical expenses they incur up to a maximum dollar amount. Also known as *reimbursement benefits.*

indemnity reinsurance. A type of reinsurance used to effect, in most cases, a partial transfer of business and to form a basis for sharing the risks of the insurance business. *Contrast with* **assumption reinsurance.** *See also* **reinsurance.**

independent audit. *See* **external audit.**

independent insurance agent. A licensed sales professional who is not under contract to one insurer but is authorized to market the products of a number of companies.

indeterminate premium life insurance policy. A type of nonparticipating whole life policy that specifies two premium rates—both
a maximum guaranteed rate and a lower rate. The insurer
charges the lower premium rate when the policy is purchased
and guarantees that rate for at least a stated period of time, after
which the insurer uses its actual mortality, interest, and expense
experience to establish a new premium rate that may be higher
or lower than the previous premium rate. Also known as
nonguaranteed premium life insurance policy and *variable-
premium life insurance policy.*

index. A statistical measurement system that tracks the performance
of a group of similar investments.

index-number trend analysis. *See* **trend analysis.**

indirect cost. In accounting, a cost that cannot be physically traced
to one specific product, line of business, department, or other
cost object. Also known as *overhead costs. Contrast with* **direct
cost.**

**Individual Accident and Sickness Insurance Minimum Standards
Act.** In the United States, a National Association of Insurance
Commissioners (NAIC) model law that establishes minimum
standards for all individual health policies other than Medicare
supplement policies.

individual cession administration. A method of reinsurance administration in which the assuming company administers the reinsurance and bills the ceding company for the individual lives
reinsured. The ceding company provides the assuming company
with detailed information about individual policies and informs
the assuming company of any changes that affect the
reinsurance.

individual insurance policy. An insurance policy that is issued to
insure the life or health of a named person. Some individual
policies also provide insurance coverage for the named person's
immediate family or a second named person. *Contrast with*
group insurance.

individual level cost allocation methods. Pension plan valuation
methods that measure costs for individual participants and sum
the individual costs to obtain costs for the plan as a whole. Also
known as *individual level-premium cost methods. Contrast with*
aggregate level cost allocation methods.

individual level-premium cost methods. *See* **individual level cost allocation methods.**

individual policy pension trust. A type of allocated pension plan funding arrangement under which plan trustees purchase individual level premium annuity contracts for each member of the plan. *See also* **allocated pension funding contract.**

individual practice association (IPA) model. A type of open panel health maintenance organization (HMO) that contracts with an association of physicians, known as an IPA, that agrees to provide services for the HMO's subscribers. *See also* **open panel HMO.**

individual retirement account. *See* **individual retirement arrangement (IRA).**

individual retirement annuity. In the United States, an individual deferred annuity that qualifies for favorable federal income tax treatment because it meets requirements specified in the federal tax laws for individual retirement arrangements. *See also* **individual retirement arrangement (IRA).**

individual retirement arrangement (IRA). In the United States, a retirement savings plan that allows people with earned income to deposit a portion of that income in a tax-deferred savings arrangement that is established by an individual and that meets certain requirements specified in the federal tax laws, including a requirement that the trustee of the trust account be a bank, insurance company, or other financial institution. *See also* **Keogh plan.**

individual stop-loss coverage. A type of stop-loss insurance coverage purchased by self-insured employers that provides benefits to the employer when a health claim is in excess of a stated amount. Also known as *specific stop-loss coverage*. *See also* **aggregate stop-loss coverage.**

industrial insurance. A form of life insurance characterized by (1) death benefits of $2,000 or less, (2) a weekly or monthly premium payment schedule, (3) the collection of renewal premiums at the policyowner's home by an agent, and (4) minimum underwriting requirements. Although industrial insurance is no longer a popular insurance product, the home service distribution method that was used to sell industrial insurance is still used today to sell a variety of insurance products. Also known as *debit insurance*. *See also* **home service distribution system.**

inflation. An increase in the average price level of goods and services during a specified period.

inflation protection rider. A long-term care (LTC) policy rider that either automatically increases the benefit amount by a specified percentage each year, or allows the insured to opt for a higher daily benefit at specified intervals during the lifetime of a policy, without having to show evidence of insurability. *See also* **long-term (LTC) insurance.**

inflation risk. The risk that the average price level of goods and services will increase during a specified period.

informal contract. A contract that is enforceable because the parties to the contract met requirements concerning the substance of the agreement rather than requirements concerning the form of the agreement. For example, an oral contract is an example of an informal contract. *Contrast with* **formal contract.**

information systems. The function within a business organization that facilitates data processing and enables the resulting information to be made available to employees who need it. Also known as *information technology.*

inside director. A member of a business organization's board of directors who holds a position with the company in addition to the position on the board. *Contrast with* **outside director.**

insolvency. (1) The inability of a business organization to pay its financial obligations as they come due. (2) For an insurer, the inability to maintain capital and surplus above the minimum standard of capital and surplus required by law.

inspection report. A type of investigative consumer report that is developed by a consumer reporting agency for an insurer to use during the underwriting process. The inspection report is compiled from public records and sometimes from interviews with the proposed insured; and contains information about a proposed insured's lifestyle, occupation, and financial status. *Contrast with* **investigative consumer report.**

installment certificate. A document that is given to the beneficiary of a life insurance policy that describes how a life insurance policy's proceeds are to be paid under a settlement option. *See also* **settlement option.**

institutional advertising. A form of advertising that promotes an idea, a philosophy, an organization, or an industry, rather than a specific product or service.

instrumental activities of daily living (IADLs). In long-term care (LTC) insurance, activities that require higher levels of functional ability than basic activities of daily living and provide an indication of whether a person is able to function independently at home. The IADLs include the ability to use a telephone, use transportation services, shop for groceries, prepare meals, perform housework tasks, and take medicine as directed by a prescribing physician. *See also* **activities of daily living (ADLs).**

insurable interest. In insurance, a person exhibits an insurable interest in a potential loss if that person will suffer a genuine economic loss if the event insured against occurs. Without the presence of insurable interest, an insurance contract is not formed for a lawful purpose and, thus, is not a valid contract.

insurance. A mechanism for transferring the risk of financial loss from events such as fire, accident, illness, or death from an individual or entity to an insurance company.

Insurance Act. In Canada, a general statute that contains most of the insurance law of a common law province and that regulates the conduct of insurers and insurance agents within the province.

insurance agent. A person who is authorized by an insurance company to represent that company in its dealings with applicants for insurance. Also known as *sales agent. Contrast with* **broker.** *See also* **captive agent.**

insurance broker. *See* **broker.**

insurance commissioner. In the United States, the individual who is responsible for directing the operations of a state insurance department. Also known as *superintendent of insurance* and *director of insurance.*

Insurance Companies Act. The Canadian legislation that sets out federal insurance laws and the regulatory system for federally regulated life insurance companies.

insurance fraud. Any fraud that involves an insurance company, whether committed by consumers, insurance company employees, agents, health care providers, or anyone else connected with an insurance transaction.

Insurance Fraud Prevention Model Act. In the United States, a National Association of Insurance Commissioners (NAIC) model law that promotes the full utilization of the expertise of the insurance commissioner to investigate and discover fraudulent insurance acts, halt fraudulent insurance acts, and assist and receive assistance from state, local, and federal law enforcement and regulatory agencies in enforcing laws prohibiting fraudulent insurance acts.

Insurance Holding Company Acts. Laws in effect in most states that control and monitor acquisitions of insurance companies. According to these laws, any company proposing to acquire control of an insurer must file with that insurer's home state a comprehensive application for approval and allow regulators to routinely monitor the members of holding company systems so as to guard against inappropriate transfers of funds.

Insurance Information and Privacy Protection Model Act. In the United States, a National Association of Insurance Commissioners (NAIC) model act that establishes standards for the collection, use, and disclosure of information gathered in connection with insurance transactions. Also known as *NAIC Model Privacy Act*.

insurance leverage ratio. A financial ratio used to measure an insurer's debt burden in relationship to the resources it has available to support the debt burden. The ratio compares an insurer's contractual reserves with its capital and/or surplus.

Insurance Marketplace Standards Association (IMSA). In the United States, an independent, voluntary association of insurance companies formed to promote high ethical standards in advertising, sales, and service of individual life insurance and annuity products. IMSA's program incorporates a set of ethical principles, a code of ethics, and a program of self-assessment and independent assessment that enables insurance companies to monitor their own compliance with regulatory requirements. *See also* **market conduct** and **market conduct laws**.

insurance producer. *See* **insurance agent.**

Insurance Regulatory Information System (IRIS). A system established and operated by the National Association of Insurance Commissioners (NAIC) in the United States to monitor the financial condition of insurers for the purposes of detecting financial distress and preventing insolvency.

insurance risk. *See* **C-2 risk (pricing risk).**

insured. A person whose life, health, property, or income is insured by an insurance policy.

insurer. The insurance company assuming the risk under an insurance contract.

insurer-administered group plan. A group insurance plan for which the insurer is responsible for handling the administrative and record-keeping aspects of the plan. *Contrast with* **self-administered group plan.**

insurer's illustrated scale. According to the National Association of Insurance Commissioners (NAIC) Life Insurance Illustrations Model Regulation in the United States, a schedule of nonguaranteed elements based on the insurer's recent experience that is included in a sales presentation for life insurance.

intangible asset. In accounting, an asset representing ownership of a legal right or other nonphysical resource. *Contrast with* **tangible asset.**

interest. Money paid for the use of money. *See also* **compound interest** and **simple interest.**

interest-adjusted cost comparison index. A cost comparison index used to compare life insurance policy costs that takes into account the time value of money. By comparing the index numbers derived for similar life insurance policies, a consumer has some basis on which to compare the costs of the policies. *See also* **net payment cost comparison index** and **surrender cost comparison index.**

interest first rule. In the United States, a federal rule governing the taxation of annuities, which states that any amount the contract owner takes out of an annuity will be considered a withdrawal of the interest (which has not been taxed), until the contract owner has withdrawn all of the interest in the contract. Also known as *earnings first rule.*

interest-indexed policy. A universal life insurance policy that provides for interest credits to be linked to an external standard, typically the *Standard & Poor's 500* (an index based on 500 select stocks).

interest maintenance reserve (IMR). For insurers in the United States, an Annual Statement account that absorbs the realized capital gains and losses in an insurer's asset portfolio caused by changes in interest rates.

interest margin. The difference between the interest rate an insurer earns on its investments and the interest rate the insurer credits to a product or assumes when pricing the product. Also known as *investment margin, interest spread,* and *spread.*

interest option. A life insurance policy settlement option under which the insurer invests the policy proceeds for the policy beneficiary or policy payee and the interest earned is periodically paid out annually, semiannually, quarterly, or monthly. *See also* **settlement options.**

interest rate. The percentage by which an amount of money is multiplied to derive the amount that is paid for the use of that money; often expressed in decimal form.

interest-rate risk. *See* **C-3 risk.**

interest-sensitive insurance. A general category of insurance products in which the face amount and/or the cash value vary according to the insurer's investment earnings.

interim insurance agreement. *See* **temporary insurance agreement (TIA).**

interim insurance law. A judicial interpretation of conditional premium receipts that generally holds that, if an insurance agent has accepted a premium payment, a proposed insured is covered until the insurer notifies the proposed insured that coverage has been terminated and returns the premium.

intermediate nursing care. In long-term care (LTC) insurance, nursing care provided on less than a 24-hour basis, usually rehabilitative in nature.

internal accounting records. Accounting records designed for financial reporting to company management, whose main interest is in having appropriate data for making decisions.

internal audit. An examination of a company's records, policies, and procedures that is conducted by the company's own employees to ensure that service standards are met, data recorded in the company's files is accurate and complete, and established procedures are being followed. *Contrast with* **external audit.**

internal customer. A company employee who receives service from other employees of the company. *Contrast with* **external customer.**

internal rate of return (IRR). In investments, the percentage rate at which an asset's earnings must be discounted, using present value techniques, in order to exactly repay the initial investment in the asset. For investments in insurance products, also known as *return on investment (ROI).*

internal replacement. *See* replacement.

Internal Revenue Service (IRS). A part of the United States Department of the Treasury that is responsible for enforcing the provisions of laws and regulations concerning income taxes in the United States.

International Accounting Standards Committee (IASC). An organization charged with promulgating accounting standards that are applicable internationally, independent of the home country of the company's financial statements.

International Classification of Diseases and Related Health Problems (ICD). One of the most commonly used codes for medical diagnoses, generally referred to as the ICD. *See also* **diagnostic and treatment codes** and **Physician's Current Procedural Terminology (CPT).**

interpleader. In the United States, a procedure under which an insurance company that cannot determine which claimant is entitled to receive insurance policy proceeds may pay the proceeds to a court and ask the court to decide the proper recipient. *See also* **payment of insurance money into court.**

intoxicants and narcotics provision. An individual health insurance policy provision which states that the insurer will not be liable for any loss resulting from the insured's being under the influence of alcohol or any narcotic unless taken on the advice of a physician.

inventory. In accounting, an itemized count and listing of a company's assets, such as property, products, materials, or securities.

invested assets. The debt securities, equity securities, and derivative securities purchased to generate earnings.

investigative consumer report. A type of consumer report that is used during the underwriting process and that is prepared by obtaining information from the consumer's neighbors, friends, associates, and others who have knowledge of the consumer's character, general reputation, personal characteristics, or mode of living. *Contrast with* **inspection report.**

investing. The practice of employing a principal sum of money—usually to purchase assets or place a sum on deposit—to generate earnings so that the principal sum will increase in value.

investment. Any expenditure of money or assets made in an attempt to earn a profit of some type.

investment adviser. A firm or individual who is compensated for providing advice to investors about the value of securities or the advisability of buying and selling securities.

Investment Adviser's Act of 1940. In the United States, a federal law that regulates the conduct of investment advisers.

investment companies. Entities that issue securities and engage primarily in investing and trading securities.

Investment Company Act of 1940. In the United States, a federal law that regulates the activities of investment companies.

investment facility contract. *See* **separate account contract.**

investment forecast. An estimate of the performance of bonds, stocks, mortgages, and other invested assets a company owns.

investment-grade bond. A bond that has been rated by a major investment advisory firm as having a low probability of default.

investment margin. *See* **interest margin.**

investment segmentation method. An insurance accounting method for allocating investment income by which an insurer uses the cash flows of a product line or line of business to purchase specific investments for that line.

Investments of Insurers Model Act (Defined Limits Version). In the United States, a National Association of Insurance Commissioners (NAIC) model law that specifies the types of assets that insurers are permitted to treat as admitted assets on their Annual Statements. It also requires the board of directors of each insurer subject to the law to adopt a written investment plan and to supervise and direct the insurer's investment function.

investment year method. *See* **new money method.**

invitation to inquire. An insurance advertisement that is designed to induce the audience to inquire further about a specific insurance policy and that contains only a brief description of the coverage provided by the policy.

IPA model. *See* **individual practice association model.**

IPG contract. *See* **immediate participation guarantee contract**

IRA. *See* **individual retirement arrangement.**

IRIS. *See* **Insurance Regulatory Information System.**

IRIS ratios. Financial ratio tests used to determine which insurance companies should have their Annual Statements scrutinized. *See also* **Insurance Regulatory Information System (IRIS), analytical phase of IRIS,** and **statistical phase of IRIS.**

IRR. *See* **internal rate of return.**

irrevocable beneficiary. A life insurance policy beneficiary who has a vested interest in the policy proceeds even during the insured's lifetime because the policyowner has the right to change the beneficiary designation only after obtaining the beneficiary's consent. *Contrast with* **revocable beneficiary.**

IRS. *See* **Internal Revenue Service.**

IRS Form 1099. In the United States, a federal tax form that insurers and other entities must provide to certain individuals who received taxable income in the previous tax year. Form 1099 shows the amount and type of disbursement, the taxable amount, and the amount of tax withheld. This information must also be provided to the Internal Revenue Service (IRS) and appropriate state tax authority.

IRS Form 5498. In the United States, a federal tax form insurers must provide to annuity contract owners by May 31 of each year for each individual retirement annuity. Form 5498 shows the fair market value of the annuity and the amount and type of contributions made to the annuity during the previous tax year. The insurer also provides the information on the form to the Internal Revenue Service (IRS) and state tax authority.

issue strain. *See* **surplus strain.**

jet unit underwriting. A method used to organize underwriting work that establishes a group of two to four employees who screen insurance applications and approve for immediate policy issue those applications that meet certain well-defined criteria. Similar method also used for organizing the work of the claim area.

joint and survivor annuity. An annuity under which the insurer agrees to make a series of benefit payments to two or more individuals until both or all of the individuals die. Also known as *joint and last survivorship annuity*.

joint life annuity. A type of annuity contract that covers more than one life and pays benefits until one of the covered people dies.

joint life insurance. Insurance policies that offer benefits for two or more lives, payable on the first death, the second death, or upon each death. Also known as *first-to-die life insurance* and *joint-and-last survivor insurance*.

joint venture. A type of partnership arrangement between two otherwise independent businesses that agree to undertake a specific project together for a specified time period.

joint whole life insurance. *See* **joint life insurance**.

journal entry. *See* **accounting entry**.

jumbo limit. In reinsurance, the maximum allowable dollar amount of total insurance in force and applied for with all insurers on any one life that will be automatically accepted by a reinsurer. A reinsurer is not required to automatically accept a risk that exceeds its jumbo limit and thus can reduce the likelihood of becoming over-exposed to mortality risk on any one individual life. *See also* **automatic binding limit**.

juvenile insurance policy. An insurance policy that is issued on the life of a child but is owned and paid for by an adult, usually the child's parent or legal guardian.

Keogh plan. In the United States, a qualified individual retirement arrangement (IRA) that allows self-employed persons to deposit a portion of their income earned from self- employment into a tax-deferred savings plan. Also known as *HR 10 plan*. *See also* **individual retirement arrangement (IRA).**

key person. Any person or employee whose continued participation in a business is necessary to the success of the business and whose death or disability would cause the business a significant financial loss.

key-person insurance. A type of life insurance or disability insurance that protects a business from the financial losses that occur when a key person dies or becomes disabled.

labor union group. A type of group that generally is eligible for group insurance coverage and that consists of members of a labor union or all of any class or classes of union members other than the union officials, agents, or representatives.

lapse. The termination of an insurance policy because a renewal premium is not paid by the end of the grace period.

lapse notice. *See* **policy grace notice.**

lapse rate. For a specified group of insurance contracts, a measure of the percentage of contracts that are voluntarily surrendered in a specified period, such as a year. *Contrast with* **persistency rate.**

late enrollee. For purposes of group health insurance, and according to the Health Insurance Portability and Administration Act (HIPAA) in the United States, an individual who enrolls in a group health plan other than during the first period in which he is eligible to enroll or during a special enrollment period.

late entrant. For purposes of group life and health insurance coverage, an eligible group member who enrolls for the group coverage after the expiration of her eligibility period. Unless they enroll during an open-enrollment period, late entrants generally must provide satisfactory evidence of insurability in order to enroll for group insurance coverage.

late-remittance offer. *See* **reinstatement.**

law of agency. The body of law that defines the rights, duties, and liabilities that arise among the parties when an agent represents a principal in contractual dealings with third parties. *See also* **agent** and **principal.**

layering. A method of dividing reinsurance coverage among multiple reinsurers by allowing one reinsurer or a pool of reinsurers to cover all cases in excess of an insurer's retention limit up to a specified amount. *See also* **first excess** and **second excess.**

LCM rule. *See* **lower of cost or market rule.**

legal actions provision. An individual health insurance policy provision that places limits—usually two or three years—on the time within which a claimant who disagrees with the insurer's claim decision has the right to sue the insurer to collect the amount the claimant believes is owed under the policy.

legal reserve. *See* **policy reserve.**

letter of credit. A document issued by a bank guaranteeing the payment of a customer's bank drafts up to a stated amount for a specified time period.

letters patent. In Canada, a document used by the federal government and the governments of Quebec, Manitoba, Prince Edward Island, and New Brunswick, giving an insurer the right to incorporate.

level commission schedule. A commission schedule for insurance sales that provides the same commission rate in the first policy year as in subsequent renewal policy years. *See also* **commission** and **levelized commission schedule.**

levelized commission schedule. A commission schedule for insurance sales in which first-year commissions are higher than subsequent renewal commissions, but the gap between first-year and renewal commissions is smaller than the gap in the traditional commission system. *See also* **commission** and **level commission schedule.**

level premium policies. Premiums paid for a life insurance policy or for a deferred annuity that remain the same each year that the contract is in force. *Contrast with* **modified premium policies** and **single premium policies.**

level term life insurance. Term life insurance that provides a death benefit that remains the same amount over the term of the policy.

leverage. *See* **financial leverage.**

liabilities. An accounting classification that represents a company's monetary value for its current and future obligations. An insurer's liabilities consist primarily of limited debts and vast reserves for future contractual obligations.

liability insurance. Insurance that protects the insured from financial loss when he is held legally responsible for bodily injury or property damage losses sustained by others. Also known as *casualty insurance.*

license. *See* **certificate of authority.**

LICTI. *See* **life insurance company taxable income.**

life and health insurance guaranty association. In each state in the United States, an organization that protects policyowners, insureds, beneficiaries, annuitants, payees, and assignees against losses that might result from the impairment or insolvency of a life or health insurer that does business in the state. Insurers are required to participate in a state's guaranty association in order to be licensed in that state.

Life and Health Insurance Policy Language Simplification Act. In the United States, a National Association of Insurance Commissioners (NAIC) model law that is designed to simplify the language used in individual life and health insurance policies and annuity contracts so that consumers are better able to understand the terms of their policies and contracts.

Life and Health Reinsurance Agreements Model Regulation. In the United States, a National Association of Insurance Commissioners (NAIC) model regulation providing guidelines to help determine whether enough risk is transferred in a reinsurance agreement to permit the ceding company reserve credit.

life annuity. A type of annuity contract that guarantees periodic income payments throughout the lifetime of a named individual—the *annuitant*. If a life annuity provides no further benefits after the death of the annuitant, the annuity is known as a *straight life annuity*. However, some life annuities provide that income payments will be paid either for the life of the annuitant or for a guaranteed period—*life income with period certain*—or at least until a guaranteed amount has been paid—*life income with refund annuity*. *See also* **life annuity with period certain**, **life income with refund annuity**, and **straight life annuity**.

life annuity with period certain. A type of annuity contract that guarantees periodic income payments throughout the lifetime of a named individual—the *annuitant*—and guarantees that the payments will continue for at least a specified period. If the annuitant dies before the end of that specified period, the payments will continue to be paid until the end of the period to a beneficiary designated by the annuitant. *See also* **life annuity**.

life income with refund annuity. A type of annuity contract that guarantees specified periodic income payments throughout the lifetime of a named individual—the *annuitant*—and guarantees that a refund will be made if the annuitant dies before the total of the periodic payments made equals the amount paid for the annuity. Also known as *refund annuity*. *See also* **life annuity**.

life insurance. A type of insurance that pays a benefit if the person who is insured by the contract dies while the insurance is in force.

Life Insurance and Annuities Replacement Model Regulation. In the United States, a National Association of Insurance Commissioners (NAIC) model regulation that serves as a basis for state replacement regulations and is designed to ensure that insurers and producers provide consumers with fair and accurate information about life insurance and annuity products. Also known as *Model Replacement Regulation*.

life insurance company taxable income (LICTI). The difference between a life insurance company's gross income and its tax deductions. To calculate LICTI, insurers first determine gross income, which includes advance premiums and excludes deferred and uncollected premiums.

Life Insurance Disclosure Model Regulation. In the United States, a National Association of Insurance Commissioners (NAIC) model regulation that is designed to improve purchasers' knowledge of life insurance and specific life insurance products and to enable consumers to compare the costs of life insurance policies. This regulation requires that a prospective life insurance purchaser be provided with a Buyer's Guide and a policy summary. *See also* **Buyer's Guide**, **Guide to Buying Life Insurance**, and **policy summary**.

Life Insurance Illustrations Model Regulation. In the United States, a National Association of Insurance Commissioners (NAIC) model regulation designed to protect consumers from the inappropriate or unethical use of sales illustrations by providing standards for insurers and agents to follow when they create and use illustrations to sell certain types of life insurance.

life insurance policy. *See* **life insurance**.

life insured. In all provinces of Canada except Quebec, the person whose life is insured by an individual life insurance policy.

lifetime benefit period. A feature in long-term care (LTC) insurance policies that provides for payment of a daily benefit amount for the remainder of the insured person's life, provided the insured person is receiving custodial care. *See also* **custodial care**.

lifetime maximum benefit. For a medical expense insurance policy, the maximum amount that an insurer will pay for all eligible medical expenses that an individual incurs while insured under the policy.

life with period certain annuity. *See* **life annuity with period certain**.

life with refund annuity. *See* **life income with refund annuity**.

limitation. An insurance policy provision that restricts the coverage provided by the policy. *See also* **exclusion** and **reduction**.

limited-scope regulatory examination. In the United States, a regulatory examination that focuses on specific areas of an insurer's financial condition, such as its reserves or its ability to pay claims, rather than on its financial condition as a whole. *Contrast with* **full-scope regulatory examination**. *See also* **on-site regulatory examination**.

line of business. A segment of products that has a cost pattern distinct from that of other segments. Also known as *product line*.

line of credit. A prearranged financial agreement that allows an entity to borrow money from a lender for a short term, and for up to a specified amount.

liquid assets. In accounting, a business organization's cash and readily marketable assets.

liquidation. The process of selling all company assets for cash and using that cash to pay the company's debts; any funds remaining are distributed to the owners of the business. For an insurer's liquidation, an agent of a court either (1) transfers all of the financially-troubled insurer's business and assets to other insurers or (2) sells the financially-troubled insurer's assets and terminates the business. *Contrast with* **rehabilitation.** *See also* **receivership.**

liquidation period. *See* **payout period.**

liquidity. The ease with which an asset can be converted into cash for an approximation of its true value.

liquidity ratios. Financial ratios that measure a company's ability to meet its maturing short-term obligations.

litigation. The process or act of resolving a dispute by means of a lawsuit.

loading. The total amount added to an insurance policy's net premium to cover all of the insurer's costs of doing business.

location-selling distribution system. An agency-building insurance distribution system designed to generate consumer-initiated sales at an insurance facility located in a store or other establishment at which consumers conduct personal business or shop for other products. *See also* **agency-building distribution system.**

long-term assets. In accounting, assets that a company plans to hold indefinitely or for a long time—generally more than a year—to generate income. *Contrast with* **short-term assets.**

long-term budget. A budget that generally covers periods of more than one year. *Contrast with* **short-term budget.**

long-term care (LTC) insurance. Insurance that provides medical and other services to insureds who need such care in their own homes or in an institution providing LTC care.

Long-Term Care Insurance Model Act. In the United States, a National Association of Insurance Commissioners (NAIC) model law that establishes standards for both group and individual long-term care (LTC) insurance and is designed to protect the public and, at the same time, promote the availability of LTC coverage and flexibility in the design of such coverage.

long-term disability income insurance. A type of disability income insurance that provides disability income benefits after short-term disability income benefits terminate and continues until the earlier of the date when the insured person returns to work, dies, or becomes eligible for pension benefits. *Contrast with* **short-term disability income insurance**.

long-term liabilities. In accounting, financial obligations that do not have to be paid in full during the current accounting period— usually one year. *Contrast with* **short-term liabilities**.

look-back period. In the United States, for purposes of the Health Insurance Portability and Accountability Act (HIPAA), a maximum period of six months preceding the date an individual enrolls in a group health plan during which any physical or mental condition for which medical advice, diagnosis, care, or treatment was recommended or received may be classified as a preexisting condition that is excluded from coverage for a limited period.

loss ratio. One measure of the reasonableness of health insurance policy premiums that compares the ratio of total claims incurred to total premiums received for those policies.

lower of cost or market (LCM) rule. Under statutory accounting practices, a bond's monetary value is defined as either its amortized cost or its current market value, whichever is lower.

LTC coverage. *See* **long-term care insurance**.

M&E charge. *See* **mortality and expense charge**.

mail kit. In the sale of direct response insurance products, a package that is mailed directly to a list of prospective purchasers who form an identified target market and that includes all the information and forms that a consumer needs to make a purchase decision and to apply for a policy. *See also* **direct response products and target market**.

maintenance expenses. For an insurance company, any product-related costs, including renewal commissions and some agency expenses, that are incurred after an insurance contract is in force and that are necessary to keep a policy in force. Also known as *renewal expenses*.

maintenance fee. A fee that insurers charge to the owners of variable annuities to pay for administration of the contract, including preparation of statements, premium notices, mailings, and other customer services. The fee is typically a flat fee that is deducted pro rata from the various accounts in proportion to the assets in the accounts.

major medical insurance plan. Traditional medical expense insurance plan that provides substantial benefits for insureds' hospital expenses, surgical expenses, and physicians' fees.

managed health care plan. A medical expense insurance plan that combines the financing and delivery of health care within a system that seeks to control the cost, accessibility, and quality of care. Insureds within such plans typically must use, or are provided incentives to use, the health care providers managed, owned, or under contract with the health insurance provider. *See also* **preferred provider arrangement (PPA)** and **preferred provider organization (PPO)**.

management accounting. The process of identifying, measuring, analyzing, and communicating financial information.

management by exception (MBE). A management principle stating that managers should be informed about an operational activity only when a result differs by a specified monetary amount or a specified percentage from what was expected.

manager of agency operations. The person who heads an insurer's agency operations unit and who serves as the primary link between the home office and the insurer's field offices. *See also* **home office** and **field office**.

mandated benefits. In the United States, benefits required by state law to be provided by health insurance policies, including coverage for newborn and handicapped children, alcoholism and substance abuse treatment, and the treatment of mental illness.

manual rating. A method of calculating group insurance premium rates for broad classes of groups, especially for groups with no credible claim experience. In manual rating, the insurer uses its own past experience—and sometimes the experience of other insurers—to estimate a group's expected claims and expense experience. *See also* **experience rating**.

margin. *See* **net income**.

marginal cost. In accounting, the additional total expense incurred as a result of producing one additional unit of an existing product or service. Also known as *incremental cost.*

market. A group of people who are actual or potential buyers of a product. *See also* **target market.**

market conduct. The general term that insurers and regulators use to designate the area of insurer activity involving advertising, sales, and distribution of insurance products.

market conduct examination. In the United States, a type of routine on-site regulatory investigation in which state insurance regulators verify that, in its dealings with customers, the insurer is complying with all applicable statutes and regulations regarding sales, advertising, underwriting, and claims. *Contrast with* **financial condition examination.** *See also* **on-site regulatory examination.**

market conduct laws. State insurance laws that are designed to ensure that insurance companies conduct their businesses fairly and ethically.

marketing. The way a business organization identifies its customers, defines and develops the products or services that its customers want, and sells and distributes those products or services to customers.

marketing function. The functional area within a business organization that conducts and organizes the company's sale and distribution of products and services.

market risk. For investors, the risk associated with fluctuations in stock prices.

market value. *See* **current market value.**

market value adjusted annuity. An annuity product that features fixed interest rate guarantees combined with an interest rate adjustment factor that can cause the surrender value to fluctuate in response to market conditions.

master application. In group insurance, a document that contains the specific provisions of the plan of insurance being applied for and that is signed by an authorized officer of the proposed policyholder.

master budget. In accounting, the overall operating and financing plans for a company during a specified accounting period. Also known as *performance plan*.

master group insurance contract. In group insurance, the legal document certifying the relationship between the insurer and the group policyholder and insuring a number of people under one contract. *See also* **certificate of insurance.**

matching principle. In accounting, an expense recognition concept which states that a company should recognize expenses as the company earns the revenues related to those expenses, regardless of when the company receives payment for the revenues earned.

material misrepresentation. (1) In general contract law, a misrepresentation of the facts by a contracting party that induces another party to enter into a contract when, had the truth been known, he would not have done so. (2) In insurance law, a misrepresentation of the facts by an insurance applicant that is relevant to the insurer's evaluation of a proposed insured.

materiality. Relevancy. (1) In insurance law, all facts that affect an insurer's risk-appraisal decision. (2) In accounting, the quality of accounting information that requires companies to disclose all significant information in their financial statements.

maturity date. (1) For endowment in insurance, the date on which an insurer will pay the face amount of an endowment policy to the policyowner if the insured is still living. (2) In investing, the date on which a bond issuer must repay to the bondholder the amount originally borrowed. (3) For an annuity, the date on which the insurer begins to make annuity payments. Also known as *income date*.

maturity value. *See* **bond principal.**

maximum benefit period. In insurance, the maximum length of time during which benefits will be paid under an insurance contract.

MBE. *See* **management by exception.**

McCarran-Ferguson Act. A U.S. federal law under which Congress agreed to leave insurance regulation to the states as long as Congress considered state regulation to be adequate.

MCCSR. *See* **Minimum Continuing Capital and Surplus Requirements.**

MDO policy. *See* **monthly debit ordinary policy.**

measuring-unit concept. An accounting principle which states that a company should record its accounting information in monetary terms, such as U.S. dollars or Canadian dollars.

mediation. A conflict resolution method in which an impartial third party facilitates negotiations between conflicting parties in an effort to create a mutually agreeable resolution to the dispute.

Medicaid. In the United States, a joint federal and state medical insurance program administered by the states to provide payment for health care services, including long-term care, for people with low incomes.

medical expense insurance. A type of health insurance coverage that pays benefits for all or part of the treatment of an insured's sickness or injury. *See also* **health insurance.**

Medical Information Bureau. *See* **MIB, Inc.**

medical necessity. A health insurance policy criterion requiring that a prescribed medical procedure be one that (1) is considered effective and that is normally used for the specified illness or injury and (2) does not exceed in scope, duration, or intensity the level of care needed to provide safe, adequate, and appropriate diagnosis or treatment.

medical report. The portion of an insurance application designed to be completed by both the proposed insured and a physician. A physician records the proposed insured's answers to health history questions and records the results of a medical examination given to the proposed insured. In life insurance, the medical report is known as Part II of the insurance application. *See also* **paramedical report** and **Part II.**

medical savings account (MSA). In the United States, a trust that is created for the purpose of paying the trust account holder's qualified medical expenses and that provides the account holder with certain tax advantages.

Medicare. A U.S. government health insurance plan that provides hospital, medical, and surgical benefits for persons age 65 and older and people with certain disabilities. Medicare Part A provides basic hospital insurance and Medicare Part B provides benefits for physicians' professional services.

Medicare supplement insurance. In the United States, health insurance coverage designed to provide benefits for certain expenses not covered under Medicare, such as Medicare deductible amounts and copayments. This coverage is available only to individuals who are covered by Medicare. Also known as *Medigap insurance. See also* **Medicare.**

Medigap insurance. *See* **Medicare supplement insurance.**

membership rights. In a mutual insurance company, ownership rights, such as the right to vote in elections for the company's board of directors on the basis of one vote for each policyowner. *See also* **mutual insurance company.**

memorandum of association. In Canada, a document similar to letters patent that contains the fundamental terms for registering for incorporation in the provinces of British Columbia, Alberta, Saskatchewan, Ontario, Newfoundland, or Nova Scotia.

Mental Health Parity Act of 1996. In the United States, federal legislation that requires group health plans that offer medical and mental health benefits to establish the same annual and lifetime dollar limits for both mental health benefits and medical health benefits.

merger. A legal transaction joining two corporations to form a distinct new corporation.

MGA. *See* **modified guaranteed annuity.**

MIB, Inc. A nonprofit organization established to provide information to insurers about impairments that applicants have admitted to, or that other insurers have detected, in connection with previous applications for insurance. Formerly known as *Medical Information Bureau.*

minimum capital and surplus requirements. Solvency requirements, established by each jurisdiction's regulators, that set specific minimum dollar amounts of capital and surplus for an insurer as a whole and for each of the company's product lines. Also known as *statutory minimum capitalization requirements.*

minimum cash balance. The amount of cash that a business organization determines is necessary to pay all obligations in a specified accounting period without having excess cash. Also, the monetary amount that a bank requires an account holder to keep in a given account at all times.

minimum cession. A statement in a reinsurance treaty describing the smallest amount of risk that an insurer will cede.

Minimum Continuing Capital and Surplus Requirements (MCCSR). In Canada, risk-based capital requirements that federally licensed insurers must meet in order to be considered solvent. The MCCSR are similar to the National Association of Insurance Commissioners (NAIC) risk-based capital (RBC) ratio requirements in the United States.

minimum death benefit guarantee. Statement included in variable annuities specifying that, if the contract owner dies before the annuity payments begin, the named beneficiary will receive a benefit equal to the greater of (a) the total amount of premium payments made for the annuity, less any withdrawals made, or (b) some enhanced value established as of the time of the contract owner's death.

minimum distribution. *See* **required minimum distribution (RMDs).**

minimum guaranteed interest rate. For a fixed annuity or a variable annuity's fixed account, the interest rate—typically three or four percent—that an insurance company contractually agrees that it will pay on the principal balance.

minimum premium plan (MPP). A group health insurance funding mechanism under which the group policyholder deposits into a special account funds that are sufficient to pay a stated amount of expected claims, and the insurer administers the plan and pays claims from that special account until the funds are exhausted. Thereafter, the insurer is responsible for paying claims from its own funds, and it charges the policyholder a premium for the coverage provided. *See also* **administrative services only (ASO) contract** and **self-insured group insurance plan.**

minimum required distributions (MRDs). *See* **required minimum distributions (RMDs).**

Minimum Reserve Standards for Individual and Group Health Insurance Contracts. A National Association of Insurance Commissioners (NAIC) model law that establishes minimum reserve standards for all types of individual and group health insurance products except Medicare supplement and long-term care policies.

minor. A person who has not attained the legal age of majority and, thus, has limited contractual capacity.

misrepresentation. A false or misleading statement. (1) In insurance sales, a false or misleading statement made by a sales agent to induce a customer to purchase insurance is a prohibited sales practice. (2) In insurance underwriting, a false or misleading statement by an insurance applicant may provide a basis for the insurer to avoid the policy.

misstatement of age or sex provision. A life insurance, health insurance, and annuity policy provision that describes how policy benefits will be adjusted if the age or sex of the insured has been misstated in the insurance application. Typically, the benefits payable will be those that the premiums paid would have purchased for the correct age or sex.

MLA system. *See* **multiple-line agency system.**

modco. *See* **modified coinsurance.**

model act. *See* **model bill.**

Model Annuity and Deposit Fund Disclosure Regulation. *See* **Annuity Disclosure Model Regulation.**

model bill. A sample law that is developed by a national association of state or provincial regulators and that the states or provinces are encouraged to use as a basis for their laws. In the United States, the National Association of Insurance Commissioners (NAIC) proposes model insurance laws, and in Canada, the Canadian Council of Insurance Regulators (CCIR) proposes such laws.

Model Hazardous Condition Regulation. In the United States, a National Association of Insurance Commissioners (NAIC) model regulation that gives the insurance commissioner of an insurer's state of domicile the authority to order the insurer to take specified actions to improve its financial condition.

Model Law on Examinations. In the United States, a National Association of Insurance Commissioners (NAIC) model law that requires each insurer domiciled in the state to undergo a financial condition examination at least every five years.

Model Newborn Children Bill. In the United States, a National Association of Insurance Commissioners (NAIC) model law that requires health insurance policies that provide coverage for a family member of the insured to provide coverage for a newly born child of the insured from the moment of birth.

Model Policy Loan Interest Rate Bill. In the United States, a National Association of Insurance Commissioners (NAIC) model law that places a maximum limit on the interest rate that may be charged on policy loans and requires insurers to state the applicable interest rate in their policies.

Model Privacy Act. *See* **Insurance Information and Privacy Protection Model Act.**

model regulation. *See* **model bill.**

Model Regulation for Complaint Records to be Maintained Pursuant to the NAIC Unfair Trade Practices Act. In the United States, a National Association of Insurance Commissioners (NAIC) model regulation that describes the minimum information that insurers must include in their complaint records and sets forth a sample format for a complaint record.

Model Regulation to Eliminate Unfair Sex Discrimination. In the United States, an National Association of Insurance Commissioners (NAIC) model regulation that prohibits life and health insurers from denying benefits or coverage on the basis of a proposed insured's sex and/or marital status.

Model Replacement Regulation. *See* **Life Insurance and Annuities Replacement Model Regulation.**

modified coinsurance (modco). A type of proportional reinsurance in which the ceding company maintains the entire reserve for each policy. *See also* **ceding company** and **reinsurer.**

modified coverage policy. A whole life insurance policy under which the amount of insurance provided decreases by specific percentages or amounts either when the insured reaches certain stated ages or at the end of stated time periods.

modified guaranteed annuity (MGA). A deferred annuity for which the underlying assets are held in a separate account, but the contract values are guaranteed if held for a specific time.

modified opinion. In accounting, an auditor's opinion that contains explanatory language concerning specified circumstances, such as material inconsistencies resulting from a change in accounting principles or practices.

modified premium policies. An insurance policy for which the policyowner first pays a lower premium than she would for a similar level-premium policy for a specified initial period and then pays a higher premium than she would for a similar level-premium policy. *Contrast with* **level premium policies** and **single premium policies.**

modified reserve. A type of contractual reserve an insurer develops using a modified reserve valuation method that permits an insurer to set a lower-than-level first-year contractual reserve in recognition of the surplus strain from a product's first-year expenses.

money market fund. An investment fund that achieves great liquidity by investing in short-term, securities offering low returns and little investment risk.

money market subaccount. One of the three main asset classes in an insurance company's separate account within which owners of variable annuity contracts can deposit funds and have the funds invested in short-term money instruments or cash equivalents, such as bank certificates of deposit (CDs) and United States Treasury bills. *See also* **bond subaccount** and **stock subaccount.**

money purchase plan. *See* **defined contribution pension plan.**

monthly debit ordinary (MDO) life insurance. A whole life insurance policy that is marketed through the home service distribution system and is paid for by monthly premium payments. *See also* **home service distribution system.**

moral hazard. The possibility that a person may act dishonestly in an insurance transaction.

morbidity. The relative incidence of sickness and injury occurring among a given group of people. *Contrast with* **mortality.**

morbidity rate. The rate at which sickness and injury occur within a defined group of people. Insurers base health insurance premiums in part on the morbidity rate for a proposed insured's age group. *Contrast with* **mortality rate.**

morbidity table. A chart that shows the rates of sickness and injury occurring among given groups of people categorized by age. *Contrast with* **mortality table.**

mortality. The relative incidence of death occurring among a given group of people. *Contrast with* **morbidity.**

mortality and expense risks (M&E) charge. A variable annuity fee designed to cover various risks and expenses assumed by the insurer, including the risk involved in providing the annuity death benefit and certain other guarantees. Generally, the M&E charge is calculated as a percentage of the assets held by the investment funds underlying the various subaccounts

mortality experience. The number or rate of deaths that actually occur in a given group of people. *Contrast with* **expected mortality.**

mortality margin. A favorable difference between an insurer's actual mortality experience and the expected mortality used in the technical design of an insurance product. A type of profit margin.

mortality rate. A percentage rate at which death occurs among a defined group of people of a specified age and sometimes of a specified gender. Insurers base the premiums for life insurance in part on the mortality rate for a proposed insured's age group. *Contrast with* **morbidity rate.**

mortality risk. (1) The likelihood that a life insured will die sooner than statistically expected. (2) The likelihood that an annuitant will live longer than statistically expected.

mortality table. A chart that shows the expected death rates among a particular group at each age—that is, how many of the people in each age group may be expected to die in a given year. *Contrast with* **morbidity table.**

mortality table with projection. A chart used in life insurance product design and premium pricing showing mortality rates that an insurer has modified by multiplying them by a chosen percentage. *Contrast with* **static mortality table.**

mortgage. A loan secured by a pledge of specified real property.

mortgage redemption insurance. A plan of decreasing term life insurance designed to provide a death benefit amount that corresponds to the decreasing amount owed on a mortgage loan.

motor vehicle record (MVR). In the United States, a record that typically contains information about a person's driving history, including information about traffic violations and arrests and convictions for driving-related incidents.

Movement of Securities Return. A statement that each federally-licensed insurer in Canada must file every six months with the Office of the Superintendent of Financial Institutions (OSFI). The statement lists all of the securities that the insurer bought and sold during the preceding six-month period and all of the insurer's loans, including its policy loans, for that period.

moving average market method. An accounting process in which an insurer in Canada systematically adjusts unrealized gains or losses that result from changes in the current market value of equity investments over a period of years.

MPP. *See* **minimum premium plan.**

MRDs. *See* **minimum required distributions.**

MSA. *See* **medical savings account.**

multiple employer group. A type of group that generally is eligible for group insurance coverage and that consists of employees of (1) two or more employers, (2) two or more labor unions, or (3) one or more employers and one or more labor unions.

multiple-line agency (MLA) system. An agency-building insurance distribution system that uses full-time career agents and agent-brokers to distribute life, health, and property/casualty insurance products for a group of affiliated insurance companies. The MLA system offers a more comprehensive product line than the ordinary system. *See also* **agency-building distribution system.**

mutual benefit method. A method used in the past to fund life insurance in which the participating members of a mutual benefit society agreed to pay an equal, specific amount of money after the death of any other member. Also known as *post-death assessment method.*

mutual fund. An account established by a financial services company that combines the money of many people and invests it in a variety of financial instruments.

mutual insurance company. An insurance company that is owned by its policyowners. *Contrast with* **stock insurance company.**

mutualization. The process of converting a stock insurance company's corporate form of organization to that of a mutual company. *See also* **mutual insurance company, demutualization,** and **stock insurance company.**

MVR. *See* **motor vehicle record.**

NAIC. *See* **National Association of Insurance Commissioners.**

NAIC accreditation program. A program sponsored by the National Association of Insurance Commissioners (NAIC) in the United States to provide a method for states to demonstrate that their solvency regulation systems meet specified minimum standards so that other states can be confident those regulatory systems are adequate and effective.

NAIC standard complaint form. A form that state insurance departments use to provide the National Association of Insurance Commissioners (NAIC) with information about complaints received from consumers about insurers.

named-perils policy. A type of homeowner's insurance policy that covers losses caused only by specific perils named in the policy.

NAR. *See* **net amount at risk.**

NASD. *See* **National Association of Securities Dealers.**

NASD Conduct Rules. Rules adopted by the National Association of Securities Dealers (NASD) to define how members and their registered principals and representatives must conduct their business.

NASD Series 6 examination. An examination administered by the National Association of Securities Dealers (NASD) that tests knowledge of securities transactions. In U.S. insurance companies, all personnel who sell variable insurance products must pass the Series 6 examination.

National Association of Insurance Commissioners (NAIC). A private, nonprofit association of insurance commissioners from all 50 states and the District of Columbia that promotes uniformity of state insurance regulation within the United States. The NAIC adopts model bills and regulations which each state can choose to adopt, use as the basis for its own laws and regulations, or ignore altogether.

National Association of Securities Dealers (NASD). In the United States, a nonprofit organization of securities brokers and dealers that promotes fair and ethical practices in the securities business.

national bank. A commercial bank that operates under a charter granted by a federal regulatory agency and is subject to regulation and supervision by federal regulators.

National Conference of Insurance Legislators (NCOIL). An organization in the United States that was formed to help educate state legislators on insurance issues, improve the quality of state insurance regulation, make insurance more affordable, and work to ensure that insurance regulation remains with the states.

National Organization of Life and Health Guaranty Associations (NOLHGA). In the United States, an organization to which most state guaranty associations belong; its primary function is to facilitate communications among the various state guaranty associations. *See also* **guaranty association.**

National Securities Clearing Corporation (NSCC). An organization that serves as a middleman for the electronic transmission of data between issuers of securities and retail sellers of securities. The NSCC is the most widely used securities clearinghouse for variable annuities and is a dominant presence in the field of transaction clearing for stocks, bonds, and mutual funds.

NAV. *See* **net asset value.**

NCOIL. *See* **National Conference of Insurance Legislators.**

needs analysis. The sales process of developing a detailed personal and financial picture of a customer in order to evaluate the customer's financial needs.

net amount at risk. An insurer's exposure to financial loss under a given life insurance policy. The difference between the face amount of a life insurance policy—other than a universal life policy—and the policy reserve the insurer has established at the end of any given policy year.

net annuity cost. A monetary amount equal to the present value of future periodic payments under an annuity contract, calculated on a net basis, without any specific provision for expense loading. *Contrast with* **gross annuity cost.** *See also* **annuity cost.**

net asset value (NAV). The value of one share in a mutual fund.

net cash value. *See* **cash surrender value.**

net change in cash. In accounting, an increase or decrease in cash during an accounting period.

net GAAP reserves. An insurer's reported GAAP reserves minus deferred acquisition costs (DAC). Net GAAP reserves are similar to modified statutory reserves in that both net GAAP reserves and modified statutory reserves represent the insurer's contractual reserve liabilities modified by an allowance for the high cost of first-year expenses. *See also* **GAAP accounting records** and **deferred acquisition costs.**

net income. For a business organization, any money that remains from the company's sales revenues after deductions have been made for sales costs, operating expenses, and taxes. Also known as *profit, profit margin,* and *spread. Contrast with* **net loss.**

net level annual premium (NLAP). In insurance product pricing, one premium in a stream of equal *annual* payments all having a present value equal to a given net single premium. *See also* **net single premium.**

net loss. For a business organization, the amount of a company's expenses (sales costs, operating expenses, and taxes) for a reporting period that exceeds its revenues for the period. *Contrast with* **net income.**

net payment cost comparison index. A cost comparison index used to compare life insurance policies that takes into account the time value of money and that measures the cost of a policy over a 10- or 20-year period assuming the policyowner pays premiums over the entire period. *Contrast with* **surrender cost comparison index.**

net premium. The amount of money an insurer needs to receive for an insurance policy in order to provide for a product's expected cost of benefits. No loading for expenses is added to this amount. *Contrast with* **gross premium.** *See also* **loading.**

net reserve. For an insurance company, any reserve that is developed without explicitly taking into consideration an insurer's product-related expenses. A reserve developed using a net reserve valuation method. *Contrast with* **gross reserve.**

net reserve valuation method. A method of computing reserves which does not make explicit provision for product-related expenses or loading.

net single premium (NSP). For a life insurance or an immediate annuity product, the actuarial present value at the time of issue of the product's total expected future cost of benefits.

net worth. In accounting, the difference between a person's or an organization's assets and liabilities.

netting off. In a reinsurance arrangement, a process by which a ceding company subtracts the claim amount owed to it by a reinsurer from the amount that the ceding company owes the reinsurer for premiums.

network. In a managed health care plan, the health care providers with which the managed care plan negotiates fees and contracts for services. *See also* **managed health care plan.**

Newborns' and Mothers' Health Protection Act of 1996. In the United States, federal legislation that requires group health plans offering coverage for hospital stays related to childbirth to provide coverage for at least a minimum number of days.

new business. For insurance purposes, the general term used to describe all the activities required to market insurance, submit applications for insurance, evaluate the risks associated with those applications, and issue and deliver insurance policies.

new business strain. *See* **surplus strain.**

new money method. An accounting method that insurers use for deferred annuities that credits the account with the interest rate that is in effect at the time of each premium payment, so that different interest rates are credited to various portions of the money in the annuity account. *Contrast with* **portfolio method.**

NLAP. *See* **net level annual premium.**

NOLHGA. *See* **National Organization of Life and Health Guaranty Associations.**

no-load fund. A mutual fund that does not charge a sales commission when shares are bought. *See also* **back-end load** and **front-end load.**

no-load policy. Life insurance policies or annuities for which an insurer makes no deduction from premium payments for charges or policy issuance.

nominal account. *See* **temporary account.**

nominal interest rate. An interest rate that is quoted contractually by a lender or a borrower and does not take into account the effects of compounding. The nominal interest rate will always be less than the effective interest rate. Also known as *stated interest rate*. *Contrast with* **effective interest rate.**

nonadmitted assets. Assets that are reported separately from admitted assets on the Assets page of the U.S. Annual Statement and that may not be applied to support an insurer's required reserves. *Contrast with* **admitted assets.**

nonadmitted income. For insurers in the United States, income that is overdue for more than a specified period—such as three months to two years—as prescribed by state insurance laws.

nonadmitted insurer. *See* **unauthorized insurer.**

nonagency building distribution system. A type of insurance sales distribution system in which the insurer does not train, finance, or provide office facilities or support for the salespeople. The two most common types of nonagency building systems are the personal-producing general agency (PPGA) system and the brokerage distribution system. Also known as *third-party distribution system.* *Contrast with* **agency-building distribution system.** *See also* **personal-producing general agency (PPGA) system** and **brokerage distribution system.**

noncancellable and guaranteed renewable policy. An individual health insurance policy, which stipulates that, until the insured reaches a specified age (usually age 65), the insurer will not cancel the coverage, increase the premiums, or change the policy provisions as long as the premiums are paid when due. Also known as *noncancellable policy.* *Contrast with* **guaranteed renewable policy.**

noncontractual reserve. An insurer's business obligations that are not directly attributable to paying benefits for a specified product.

noncontributory plan. (1) A group insurance plan under which insured group members are not required to contribute any part of the premium for the coverage. The premiums are paid entirely by the employer or group policyholder and all eligible group members are automatically provided with coverage. (2) Retirement plans that do not require plan participants to make contributions to fund the plan. *Contrast with* **contributory plan.**

noncurrent assets. *See* **long-term assets.**

nonduplication of benefits provision. *See* **coordination of benefits (COB) provision.**

nonforfeiture options. The various ways in which a contract owner may apply the cash surrender value of an insurance or an annuity contract if the contract lapses. In the United States, the typical nonforfeiture options for life insurance are the cash payment option, the extended term insurance option, and the reduced paid-up insurance option. *See also* **cash payment option, cash surrender value, extended term insurance option,** and **reduced paid-up insurance option.**

nonguaranteed elements. The premiums, benefits, values, credits, or charges under a life insurance policy that are not guaranteed or not determined when the policy is issued.

nonmedical application. An application for insurance in which the proposed insured is not required to undergo a medical examination. However, a nonmedical application typically does contain questions that the proposed insured must answer about his or her health. *See also* **medical report, paramedical report, Part I,** and **Part II.**

nonmedical limits. The total amounts of insurance that an insurer will issue to an applicant without requiring a paramedical or medical examination.

nonmedical supplement. *See* **nonmedical application.**

nonnatural person rule. In the United States, a federal income tax rule which states that interest credited each year is currently taxable if the owner of a deferred annuity is a nonnatural person (for example, a corporation, partnership, or trust) not acting as an agent for a natural person, and if any premiums were paid after February 28, 1986.

nonpar policy. *See* **nonparticipating policy.**

nonparticipating policy. A type of insurance policy under which the policyowner does not share in the insurance company's divisible surplus by receiving policy dividends. Also known as *nonpar policy.*

nonpreferred provider. A health care provider who has not entered into a preferred provider arrangement with a health care insurer. *See also* **preferred provider arrangement (PPA).**

nonproportional reinsurance. A type of reinsurance in which neither the reinsurer nor the ceding company knows in advance what share of a risk the reinsurer will ultimately assume. *See also* **ceding company** and **reinsurer.**

nonqualified annuity. A type of annuity that does not receive all of the U.S. income tax advantages afforded qualified annuities. *Contrast with* **qualified annuity.**

nonqualified LTC plan. In the United States, a long-term care (LTC) plan issued after 1996 that does not meet the tax benefit requirements of the Health Insurance Portability and Accountability Act (HIPAA).

nonqualified retirement savings plan. In the United States, a retirement savings plan that does not meet the legal requirements necessary to qualify for favorable federal income tax treatment. In Canada, similar plans are known as *nonregistered retirement savings plans.*

nonregistered retirement savings plan. *See* **nonqualified retirement savings plan.**

nonresident corporation. *See* **foreign corporation.**

nonresident license. In the United States, an insurance license issued by a state insurance department to an individual who resides in, and is licensed by, another state.

nonsufficient funds (NSF) checks. Checks that cannot be honored by the issuing financial institution because the checking account holder did not have enough money in his or her checking account to pay the amount of the check. Also known as *bounced checks.*

non-term group life coverage. A group policy or individual policies of certain types of permanent life insurance issued to members of an employer group or other permitted group where the following criteria are met: (1) every plan of coverage was selected by the employer or other group representative; (2) some portion of the premium is paid by the group or through payroll deduction; and (3) group underwriting or simplified underwriting is used.

normal balance. In accounting, the side of an account, whether debit or credit, to which increases to the account are recorded.

normal retirement age. For a pension plan, the earliest age at which an eligible participant can retire with full benefits.

notice of claim provision. An individual health insurance policy provision that requires written notice of a claim to be given to the insurer within 20 days after the occurrence or commencement of a covered loss or as soon thereafter as is reasonably possible.

notice of expiry. A document that a reinsurer uses to notify the ceding company that an offer to reinsure is due to expire and to request additional information, a cession, a drop notice, or an extension request from the ceding company. *See also* **ceding company**, **cession**, and **reinsurer**.

notice of transfer. A written document that provides policyowners affected by an assumption reinsurance agreement with information about the agreement and their right to consent to or reject the transfer of their policies.

notice regarding replacements. A written document that both an applicant for an insurance policy or an annuity and the sales agent must sign and submit along with the application when that policy will replace an existing one. The document gives the applicant general information about the potential effect of a replacement and advises the applicant to get all the relevant facts before making a replacement. *See also* **replacement**.

NSCC. *See* **National Securities Clearing Corporation**.

NSF checks. *See* **nonsufficient funds checks**.

NSP. *See* **net single premium**.

numerical rating system. In life insurance underwriting, a risk classification method in which each medical and nonmedical factor is assigned a numerical value based on its expected impact on mortality. *See also* **credits** and **debits**.

numeric summary. The part of a life insurance basic illustration that provides a brief overview of the amounts of a policy's death benefits, policy values, and premium outlays and contract premium (as applicable) for certain policy years. In the United States, the National Association of Insurance Commissioners (NAIC) Life Insurance Illustrations Model Regulation requires the numeric summary to follow the narrative summary in a basic illustration.

nursing home. For purposes of long-term care (LTC) insurance, a custodial facility that provides basic nonmedical care and medical care as necessary to patients.

OAS Act. *See* **Old Age Security Act**.

OASDHI Act. *See* **Old Age, Survivors, Disability and Health Insurance Act**.

OCC. *See* **Office of the Comptroller of the Currency.**

occupational rating classes. Established by insurance companies for use in underwriting disability income coverage, these classes categorize occupations according to the relative degree of risk. *See also* **underwriting.**

Office of the Comptroller of the Currency (OCC). In the United States, a bureau of the federal Department of the Treasury that is responsible for regulating national banks.

Office of the Superintendent of Financial Institutions (OSFI). In Canada, a federal regulatory agency responsible for supervising all federally chartered, licensed, or registered banks, as well as insurance, trust, loan, and investment companies.

Office of the Superintendent of Insurance. In Canada, an administrative agency established by each province to enforce the province's insurance laws and regulations.

Office of Thrift Supervision (OTS). In the United States, a bureau of the federal Department of the Treasury that is responsible for supervising all savings institutions that are insured by the Federal Deposit Insurance Corporation.

offset. In the United States, a federal tax provision that allows an insurer to use the benefits paid under one type of health insurance coverage to reduce the benefits paid under another type of coverage. The purpose of the offset is to ensure that a disabled person does not receive an excessive total amount of benefits and to encourage the disabled person to return to work.

Old Age Security (OAS) Act. A Canadian federal law that provides a monthly pension to all persons who are age 65 and older and meet specified residency requirements.

Old Age, Survivors, Disability and Health Insurance (OASDHI) Act. A U.S. federal law that protects covered individuals from loss of income resulting from retirement, death, or disability. More commonly known as Social Security. *See also* **Social Security.**

on-site regulatory examination. A tool that insurance regulators use to monitor the solvency or market conduct of insurers.

open agency. In the home service insurance distribution system, a sales territory that does not have an assigned agent because of agent promotion, transfer, or termination; usually serviced by a staff manager.

open contract. A contract that identifies the documents that constitute the contract between the parties, but the enumerated documents need not all be attached to the contract. *Contrast with* **closed contract.**

open-end credit transaction. A financial transaction in which credit is extended under an agreement in which (1) the creditor reasonably expects repeated transactions; (2) the creditor imposes a periodic finance charge on an outstanding unpaid balance; and (3) the amount of credit that may be extended to the debtor during the term of the agreement—up to any limit set by the creditor—generally is made available to the extent that any outstanding balance is repaid.

open-ended HMO. A health maintenance organization (HMO) that provides medical expense benefits to participants who use a health care provider who is not a member of the HMO's network. However, the HMO uses financial incentives to encourage participants to use network providers. Also known as *point of service (POS) plan.*

open enrollment period. In contributory group insurance plans, a short time span during which eligible people who did not choose to join the group insurance plan at the first opportunity are permitted to join by presenting only an application and without providing evidence of insurability. *See also* **eligibility period.**

open group valuation. An assessment of the value of a pension plan that takes into account the benefits of the current group of participants and hypothetical participants who may enter the plan during some limited future period. Also known as *dynamic valuation. Contrast with* **closed group valuation.**

open panel HMO. A type of health maintenance organization (HMO) that allows any physician or health care provider who meets the HMO's specific standards to contract with the HMO to provide services to HMO members. *Contrast with* **closed panel HMO.**

operating activities. Transactions that involve a company's major lines of business and that directly determine the company's net income.

operating budget. *See* **short-term budget.**

operating efficiency ratios. *See* **activity ratios.**

operating expenses. The costs that a company incurs in conducting its normal business operations.For insurers, costs other than expenses for contractual benefits. *See also* **expense.**

operational budget. A budget that includes part or all of a company's core business operations.

operational planning. The company process of determining how to accomplish specified tasks with available resources, given a company's strategic plan.

opportunity cost. For planning purposes, the benefit that is forfeited or given up in choosing one decision alternative over another.

option 1 plan. *See* **option A plan.**

option 2 plan. *See* **option B plan.**

optional insured rider. *See* **second insured rider.**

optional modes of settlement. *See* **settlement options.**

optionally renewable policy. An individual health insurance policy that gives the insurer the right to refuse to renew the policy on specified dates, to add coverage limitations, and to increase the premium rate if it does so for a class of policies. *See also* **cancellable policy, conditionally renewable policy,** and **noncancellable and guaranteed renewable policy.**

option A plan. A universal life insurance policy that provides a level death benefit amount, which is always equal to the policy's face amount. Also known as *option 1 plan.*

option B plan. A universal life insurance policy that provides a death benefit amount that, at any given time, is equal to the policy's face amount plus the amount of the policy's cash value. Also known as *option 2 plan.*

options. In finance, limited-time contracts that give the owner the right to either buy or sell a specified asset for a stated price. *See also* **payout options** and **settlement options.**

order to commence and carry on insurance business. In Canada, a document, issued by the applicable insurance regulatory body, that authorizes an insurance company to begin insuring risks.

ordinary agency distribution system. An agency-building distribution system that uses full-time career agents and agent-brokers to sell and deliver insurance and annuity products. *See also* **agency-building distribution system.**

ordinary annuity. A series of periodic payments for which the payment occurs at the end of each payment period. Also known as *annuity immediate* and *annuity in arrears. Contrast with* **annuity due.**

ordinary life insurance policy. *See* **continuous-premium whole life policy.**

original age conversion. The conversion of a term life insurance policy to a permanent plan of insurance at a premium rate that is based on the insured's age when the original term policy was purchased. *Contrast with* **attained age conversion.**

orphan policy. An insurance policy for which the original agent is no longer available to provide customer service. The original agent who sold the policy may have died, retired, or changed jobs.

OSFI. *See* **Office of the Superintendent of Financial Institutions.**

OTC market. *See* **over-the-counter market.**

OTS. *See* **Office of Thrift Supervision.**

outline of coverage. A brief description of the coverage provided by an individual health insurance policy.

out-of-pocket costs. For a health insurance plan, costs or portions of costs that an insured is required to pay that are not reimbursed by the health insurance plan.

outside director. A member of a business organization's board of directors who does not hold another position with the organization and does not own a controlling interest in the organization. *Contrast with* **inside director.**

outstanding premiums. *See* **premiums outstanding.**

overhead cost. *See* **indirect cost.**

overhead expenses. *See* **indirect cost.**

overinsurance. An amount of applied-for insurance that is excessive in relation to the potential loss for which coverage is being purchased.

overinsurance provision. An individual health insurance policy provision that defines the insurer's liability to pay policy benefits for covered losses that are insured by more than one policy. The provision is designed to ensure that a covered person will not profit from a sickness or injury. *See also* **coordination of benefits (COB) provision.**

overriding commission. An insurance sales commission that is based on the amount of sales produced by the agents in a field office. Also known as *override.*

over-the-counter (OTC) market. A way of trading securities in which dealers at different locations who have an inventory of securities stand ready to buy and sell securities through a telecommunications network that brings the buyers and sellers together.

owners' equity. *See* **capital.**

PAC system. *See* **preauthorized check system.**

package selling. An insurance sales method that involves putting a simple insurance plan into a standardized presentation and then looking for customers who can use that package of coverage.

paid-up additional insurance option. An option, available to the owners of participating life insurance policies, that allows the policyowner to use policy dividends to purchase additional insurance on the insured's life; the paid-up additional insurance is issued on the same plan as the basic policy and in whatever face amount the dividend can provide at the insured's attained age. *See also* **dividend, participating policy,** and **policy dividend options.**

paid-up policy. An insurance policy that requires no further premium payments but continues to provide coverage.

paramedical report. The portion of an insurance application designed to be completed by the proposed insured and a medical technician, a physician's assistant, or a nurse, rather than a physician. The proposed insured answers questions about his or her health history and the examiner records the results of certain physical measurements. In life insurance, the paramedical report is known as Part II of the insurance application. *See also* **medical report** and **Part II.**

par policy. *See* **participating policy.**

Part I. The section of a life insurance application that identifies the proposed insured (and the policyowner, if different from the proposed insured), specifies the amount and type of coverage requested, and provides basic insurability information. *See also* **Part II.**

Part II. The section of a life insurance application that provides medical information about the proposed insured. *See also* **medical report, paramedical report,** and **Part I.**

partial disability. *See* **residual disability.**

partial surrender provision. *See* **policy withdrawal provision.**

participating policy. A type of insurance policy that allows policyowners to receive policy dividends. Also known as *par policy. See also* **dividend.**

partnership insurance. A type of business insurance that provides cash so that the remaining partners in a business can buy the business interest of a deceased or disabled partner. *See also* **business continuation insurance plan.**

par value of a bond. *See* **bond principal.**

par value of stock. The designated legal value assigned to each outstanding share of common stock; primarily used for accounting purposes. Also known as *nominal value* and *face value.*

payback period. In capital budgeting, the number of years that must pass before the earnings a product produces equal the initial investment in the product.

payee. (1) The person or party who is to receive insurance policy proceeds in accordance with the terms of a settlement agreement. *See also* **settlement agreement.** (2) The person, usually the annuitant, who receives periodic annuity benefit payments according to the terms of an annuity contract. *See also* **annuitant.**

payment of insurance money into court. In Canada, a procedure available to insurers in the common law jurisdictions under which an insurance company that cannot determine which claimant is entitled to receive insurance policy proceeds may pay the proceeds to a court and ask the court to decide the proper recipient and thus obtain a valid discharge. In Quebec, an insurer in such a situation can obtain a valid discharge by paying the policy proceeds to the Minister of Finance. *See also* **interpleader.**

payout options. The methods available to an annuity contract owner for the distribution of the annuity's accumulated value. (1) The *lump sum distribution method* allows the contract owner to receive the balance of his account in a single payment. (2) The *fixed period option* provides that the annuity's accumulated value will be paid out over a specified period of time. (3) The *fixed amount option* provides that the annuity's accumulated value will be paid out in a preselected payment amount until the accumulated value is exhausted. (4) A *life annuity option* provides that periodic income payments will be tied in some manner to the life expectancy of a named individual. *See also* **life annuity.**

payout options provision. An annuity contract provision that grants the contract owner several choices as to how the insurer will distribute the contract's accumulated value. Also known as *settlement options provision. See also* **payout options.**

payout period. (1) The period during which a payee receives payments. (2) The period during which an insurer makes annuity benefit payments. Also known as *liquidation period* and *annuitization period.*

payroll deduction method. An automatic insurance premium payment technique whereby a policyowner's employer deducts insurance premiums directly from the employee's paycheck.

PBGC. See **Pension Benefit Guaranty Corporation.**

PCP. *See* **primary care physician.**

pension. A lifetime monthly income benefit payable to a person upon his or her retirement.

Pension Benefit Guaranty Corporation (PBGC). In the United States, a federal corporation that is responsible for guaranteeing the payment of retirement benefits for participants in defined benefit retirement plans when those plans become financially unable to pay benefits. *See also* **Employee Retirement Income Security Act (ERISA).**

Pension Benefits Act. A law enacted by the federal government and each of the provincial governments in Canada to govern the terms and operation of private pension plans.

pension fund. (1) Assets used to pay the pensions of retirees. (2) An investment management company that manages the assets used to pay the pensions of retirees.

pension plan. An agreement under which an employer or employee organization establishes a plan to provide covered employees with a lifetime monthly income benefit that begins at their retirement. The covered employees are *pension plan participants.* The entity that establishes or maintains the pension plan is the *pension plan sponsor.*

pension plan administrator. *See* **plan administrator.**

pension plan beneficiary. The individual who receives benefits under a pension plan. Current or former plan participants, as well as dependents, spouses, and survivors of plan participants, can all be pension plan beneficiaries.

pension plan document. A detailed legal agreement establishing the existence of a pension plan and specifying the rights and obligations of various parties to the pension plan.

pension plan valuation method. *See* **actuarial cost method.**

per capita beneficiary designation. A type of life insurance policy beneficiary designation in which the life insurance benefits are divided equally among the designated beneficiaries who survive the insured. For example, if the policy specifies two beneficiaries, but only one is surviving at the time of the insured's death, then the remaining beneficiary receives the entire policy benefit. *Contrast with* **per stirpes beneficiary designation.**

percentage-of-income rule. In life insurance, a rule that underwriters use to determine the amount of money an applicant can afford to spend on insurance according to the applicant's income. Insurers often stipulate that a maximum of 20 percent of an applicant's gross income can be used to buy life insurance. Also known as *20-percent rule. See also* **factor table.**

performance plan. *See* **master budget.**

period budget. A budget that covers a specific time frame, such as one month or one year, and expires at the end of that time frame.

period certain. The stated period over which an insurer makes periodic benefit payments under an annuity certain. *See also* **annuity certain.**

period certain annuity. *See* **annuity certain.**

periodic annuity payment factor. Number that shows, for annuitants at a given age, the periodic income payment amount that a contract owner can purchase for each $1,000 of single premium applied.

periodic fee. An amount that an insurer charges the owner of an unbundled insurance product, at predetermined intervals, for example, every year or month, to compensate the insurer for administrative expenses.

periodic level-premium annuity. *See* **level premium policies.**

period of confinement. In long-term care (LTC) insurance, a continuous time period during which an insured person is receiving uninterrupted long-term care at an acute hospital, a skilled nursing facility, or another inpatient facility.

permanent account. In accounting, a balance sheet account that has a balance at the beginning of each accounting period.

permanent flat extra premium. *See* **flat extra premium method.**

permanent life insurance. Life insurance that provides coverage throughout the insured's lifetime, provided premiums are paid as stated in the policy, and also provides a savings element. *Contrast with* **term life insurance.**

persistency. A measure of how long the various policies in a group of policies remain in force as a result of the continued payment of renewal premiums.

persistency bonus. A sum of money paid as compensation to an insurance agent when a policy continues in force beyond an initial period, usually five years.

persistency rate. For a specified group of insurance contracts, a measure of the percentage of contracts that remain in force during a specified period, such as a year. *Contrast with* **lapse rate.**

personal history interview (PHI). In insurance underwriting, a conversation with the proposed insured during which an underwriter clarifies information and gathers additional information needed for underwriting.

personal line of credit. *See* **line of credit.**

personal property. Any property that is not real estate, including goods such as clothing, furniture, and automobiles, and intangible items such as contractual rights. In Quebec, known as *moveable property. Contrast with* **real estate.**

personal-producing general agency (PPGA) system. A nonagency building insurance distribution system that uses personal-producing general agents to distribute insurance and annuity products. *See also* **nonagency building distribution system** and **personal-producing general agent.**

personal-producing general agent. A commissioned insurance sales agent who generally works alone, is not housed in one of an insurer's field offices, engages primarily in the sales of new policies, and holds contracts with several insurers.

personal selling distribution system. A distribution system in which commissioned or salaried salespeople sell products through verbal and written presentations made to prospective purchasers.

per stirpes beneficiary designation. A type of life insurance policy beneficiary designation in which the life insurance benefits are divided among a class of beneficiaries; for example, children of the insured. The living members of the class and the descendants of any deceased members of the class share in the benefits equally. *Contrast with* **per capita beneficiary designation.**

PHI. *See* **personal history interview.**

physical damage insurance. In property casualty insurance, coverage for losses the insured incurs due to damage to his covered automobile caused by collision or other perils.

physical examinations provision. An individual health insurance policy provision that gives the insurer the right to conduct a medical examination of the insured at the insurer's expense when reasonably necessary to the settlement of a pending claim.

Physicians' Current Procedural Terminology. One of the most commonly used codes for medical treatments that health care providers use to communicate information about medical expense claims to insurers. *See also* **diagnostic and treatment codes** and **International Classification of Diseases and Related Health Problems (ICD).**

physiological age. For a person, the relative age or youthfulness of his or her vital organs and their functioning.

plan administrator. (1) In a group insurance plan, the party responsible for handling the administrative aspects of the plan. (2) For purposes of the Employee Retirement Income and Security Act (ERISA) in the United States, the individual or organization designated in a retirement plan's summary plan description as being responsible for assuring the plan complies with applicable regulatory requirements.

plan continuation valuation. An assessment of the value of a pension plan that is based on the assumption that the plan will continue in operation. *Contrast with* **plan termination valuation**.

plan document. (1) A document that specifies the terms of a retirement plan. (2) For purposes of the Employee Retirement Income and Security Act (ERISA) in the United States, a written document by which a qualified retirement plan must be established and maintained and that describes the benefits provided by the plan, the plan's funding, and the procedure that will be followed to amend the plan.

plan participant. An employee or union member who is covered by a group retirement plan that is sponsored by the employer or union. *See also* **plan sponsor**.

plan sponsor. The employer or union that establishes a group retirement plan for the benefit of plan participants. *See also* **plan participant**.

plan termination valuation. An assessment of the value of a pension plan that is based on the assumption that the plan is being terminated as of the valuation date. *Contrast with* **plan continuation valuation**.

plan trustee. An individual or entity appointed by a qualified retirement plan sponsor who holds legal title to the retirement plan assets on behalf of the plan participants. *See also* **plan participant** and **plan sponsor**.

PNO policy. *See* **premium notice ordinary policy**.

point of service (POS) plan. *See* **open-ended HMO**.

point-to-point method. For an equity-indexed annuity, a method for crediting excess interest that involves comparing the value of the index at the start of the annuity contract term to its value at the end of the term to determine what, if any, excess interest has accrued because of a change in the index.

policy. A written document that contains the terms of the contractual agreement between an insurance company and the owner of the policy.

policy accounting. *See* **premium accounting**.

policy acquisition expenses. Any costs that an insurer incurs related to obtaining and issuing new insurance business.

policy and contract claims. An insurer's liabilities for all types of insurance policy and annuity contract claims that must be settled. Also known as *claim liabilities.*

policy anniversary. As a general rule, the date on which coverage under an insurance policy became effective.

policy benefit. *See* **benefit.**

policy charge. An amount that an insurer adds to a policy's premium or deducts from a policy's cash value in order to pay for the insurer's expenses and to provide the insurer with a profit. Also known as *policy fee.*

policy dividend. *See* **dividend.**

policy dividend options. Ways in which the owner of a participating insurance policy may receive policy dividends. *See also* **additional term insurance option, cash dividend option, dividend accumulations option, paid-up additional insurance option,** and **premium reduction option.**

policy filing. The act of submitting a contract form and any other legally required forms and documents to the insurance departments of the states and provinces where the insurance or annuity contract will be issued and sold.

policy form. A standardized contract form, drafted by an insurer and filed with insurance regulators, that shows the terms, conditions, benefits, and ownership rights of a particular insurance product.

policy grace notice. A written notification from an insurance company to a policyowner notifying the policyowner that the policy's grace period is about to expire. Also known as *lapse notice.*

policyholder. In group insurance, the employer or other type of organization that decides what kind of coverage to purchase for the group, negotiates the terms of the master contract, enters into a group insurance contract with the insurer, and usually administers part or all of the coverage. *Contrast with* **policyowner.** *See also* **group insurance.**

policy illustration. *See* **sales illustration.**

policy issue. The insurance company function that involves preparing the insurance contract, including modifying the applied-for coverage according to instructions from the underwriter, and facilitating the delivery of the policy to the customer, usually by way of the agent who sold the insurance.

policy lapse. *See* **lapse.**

policy liability. *See* **policy reserve.**

policy loan. A loan that an insurer makes to the owner of a permanent life insurance policy that is secured by the policy's cash value. When the policy's benefits are paid, the amount of any outstanding loan is deducted from the policy benefits.

policy loan provision. A provision that is included in permanent life insurance policies that build a cash value and that specifies the terms on which a policyowner may obtain a loan. *See also* **policy loan.**

policyowner. The person or other entity that enters into an individual contract of insurance with an insurer and actually owns the individual insurance policy. *Contrast with* **policyholder.**

policyowner dividend liabilities. In insurance accounting, amounts that represent all policyowner dividends that have been declared by an insurer's board of directors, but which have not yet been paid to policyowners.

policyowner dividend payment options. *See* **policy dividend options.**

policyowner service. In an insurance company, all customer service activities performed for agents and for the people or parties who own or hold insurance policies and annuities. Also known as *customer service* and *client service.*

policy premium method (PPM). A type of prospective gross level-premium reserve valuation method that is used by insurers in Canada. *See* **gross reserve valuation method** and **prospective reserve valuation method.**

policy proceeds. *See* **benefit.**

policy prospectus. *See* **prospectus.**

policy reserve. For an insurer, a liability amount that, together with future premiums and investment income, the insurer estimates it will need to pay contractual benefits as they come due under in-force policies. Policy reserves represent the insurer's obligations to customers. Also known as *contractual reserve, legal reserve,* and *statutory reserve.*

policy rider. An addition to an insurance policy that becomes a part of the insurance contract and that is as legally effective as any other part of the policy. Riders usually expand or limit the benefits payable under the contract. Also known as *endorsement.*

policy rights. The contractual rights of an insurance policy owner, such as the right to the policy values, the right to assign the values to another party, and the right to designate the beneficiary of the policy proceeds upon the death of the insured.

policy summary. A written statement that describes specific elements of the insurance policy being considered for purchase and provides the consumer with cost comparison information.

policy term. The specified period of time during which a term life insurance policy provides coverage.

policy withdrawal provision. A universal life insurance policy provision that permits the policyowner to reduce the amount in the policy's cash value by withdrawing up to the amount of the cash value in cash. Also known as *partial surrender provision.*

pooling. A method of calculating group insurance premium rates by which the insurer considers several small groups as one large group for risk assessment purposes. *Contrast with* **experience rating.**

population mortality table. A chart that shows rates of death for the general population, based on data from a population census.

portability. The degree to which an individual's insurance coverage or pension benefits can be continued when the participating individual leaves the providing benefit plan.

portfolio. In investments, a diversified collection of various securities usually assembled by an investor for the purpose of meeting a defined set of financial goals.

portfolio method. An accounting method that insurers use for deferred annuities that credits all funds in the contract owner's annuity account with one specified current rate of interest, regardless of when the money was placed in the account. *Contrast with* **new money method.**

positive leverage effect. An effect of earning a better profit due to the presence of leverage. *See also* **financial leverage** and **total leverage.**

POS plan. *See* **open-ended HMO.**

post-notice. A notice that must be sent to an insurance applicant if an underwriter denies an application or rates a policy based wholly or partially on information contained in a report from a consumer reporting agency. *See also* **consumer credit report** and **pre-notice.**

PPA. *See* **preferred provider arrangement.**

PPGA. *See* **personal producing general agency.**

PPM. *See* **policy premium method.**

PPO. *See* **preferred provider organization.**

preadmission certification. Authorization from an insurer approving nonemergency, inpatient hospital treatment. Also known as *precertification.*

precedent. A court's decision which must generally be followed by that court and the lower courts in the same jurisdiction in cases involving the same issue and substantially the same facts.

precertification. *See* **preadmission certification.**

predictive quality. A characteristic of accounting information that enables interested users to form a reasonably accurate estimate of a company's financial strength or earnings potential.

pre-existing condition. (1) According to most group health insurance policies, a condition for which an individual received medical care during the three months immediately prior to the effective date of her coverage. (2) According to most individual health insurance policies, an injury that occurred or a sickness that first appeared or manifested itself within a specified period—usually two years—before the policy was issued *and* that was not disclosed on the application for insurance.

pre-existing conditions provision. An individual and group health insurance policy provision which states that benefits will not be paid for pre-existing conditions until the insured has been covered under the policy for a specified length of time.

preference beneficiary clause. A life insurance policy provision which states that if the policyowner does not name a beneficiary, then the insurer will pay the policy proceeds in a stated order of preference. Also known as *succession beneficiary clause.*

preferred beneficiary. In Canada, a spouse, child, parent, or grandchild named as the beneficiary in any life insurance policy issued before July 1, 1962. A preferred beneficiary's written consent is required for the policyowner to change the beneficiary to anyone outside this group of family members, to obtain a policy loan, to surrender a policy, or to assign a policy. The 1962 revision of the Uniform Life Insurance Act abolished the vested rights of this class of beneficiaries.

preferred provider arrangement (PPA). A contract between a health care insurer and a health care provider or group of providers who agree to provide specified covered services to insureds.

preferred provider organization (PPO). A managed health care plan that arranges with health care providers for the delivery of health care at a discounted cost and provides incentives for PPO members to use the health care providers who have contracted with the PPO, but that also provides some coverage for services rendered by health care providers who are not part of the PPO network. *See also* **managed health care plans** and **preferred provider arrangement (PPA).**

preferred risk class. In insurance underwriting, the group of proposed insureds who represent a significantly lower than average likelihood of loss within the context of the insurer's underwriting practices. *Contrast with* **declined risk class, standard risk class,** and **substandard risk class.**

preferred stock. A type of equity security that represents ownership in a corporation that typically does not carry the voting rights of common stock, but does carry a stated dividend rate that is paid prior to any payment of common stock dividends by the same company. *Contrast with* **common stock.** *See also* **dividends.**

pre-funded inflation protection option. In a long-term care (LTC) insurance policy, a provision that guarantees that the policy's daily benefit amount will increase by a certain amount or percentage each year after the insured person reaches age 65, the cost of which is built into the policy's premium structure.

Pregnancy Discrimination Act. In the United States, a federal law that requires employers to treat pregnancy, childbirth, or related medical conditions the same as any other medical condition.

premature distributions. Withdrawals from a deferred annuity made before the contract owner is age 59½.

premium. (1) In insurance, a specified amount of money an insurer charges in exchange for the coverage provided by an insurance policy or annuity contract. (2) In reference to bond prices, the excess of a bond's market price over the bond's par value.

premium accounting. The accounting process that encompasses the maintenance of detailed accounting records and reports of insurance policy transactions. Also known as *policy accounting*.

premium bond. A bond that has a market price that is greater than the bond's principal or par value. *Contrast with* **discount bond.**

premium deposits. Amounts that an insurer's policyowners leave on deposit with the insurer to pay for future premiums.

premium income. The revenue that insurance companies receive from insurance and annuity policy sales.

premium notice ordinary (PNO) policy. In the home service insurance distribution system, an insurance policy that usually has a minimum face amount of $10,000 to $15,000, and for which premiums are paid through the mail, automatic bank draft, payroll deduction, or electronic funds transfer (EFT).

premium payment mode. For insurance policies, the frequency (monthly, quarterly, or annually) at which renewal premiums are payable.

premium receipt. A written acknowledgment that an insurer has received the initial premium submitted with an application for insurance. A premium receipt typically provides the proposed insured with some type of temporary insurance coverage while the application for insurance is being underwritten. *See also* **temporary insurance agreement.**

premium reduction option. An option, available to the owners of participating insurance policies, that allows the insurer to apply policy dividends toward the payment of renewal premiums. *See also* **dividend** and **policy dividend options.**

premiums outstanding. For Canadian insurers, individual life insurance and annuity premiums that were due on or before the Annual Return date, but for which the insurer has not yet received payment by that date. In the United States, these amounts are called *uncollected premiums*.

premium suspense account. For insurance accounting purposes, a liability account used to record transactions that are intended as premiums but which the insurer cannot accept as income until a particular event occurs.

premium tax. A tax that a state or province levies on an insurer's premium income earned within that state or province.

pre-need funeral insurance. A form of insurance that provides funds to pay for the insured's funeral and burial, which have been arranged while the insured is living. Also known as *pre-need insurance.*

pre-notice. A notice that must be given to an insurance applicant by an insurer that discloses clearly and adequately to the applicant that the insurer may use a consumer reporting agency to compile a consumer report on the insurance applicant. *See also* **consumer credit report** and **post-notice.**

preplacement. In a reinsurance arrangement, the period during which a reinsurance analyst reviews the request for coverage, establishes appropriate records and reserves facilities for the case, and follows up on reserved facilities that have been inactive for a specified period of time. *See also* **reinsurance.**

prescription drug coverage. Insurance that provides benefits for the purchase of drugs and medicines that are prescribed by a physician and that cannot be purchased without a doctor's prescription.

present value (PV). The amount of money that must be invested today in order to accumulate a specified amount of money by a certain date. *Contrast with* **future value (FV).**

present value interest factor (PVIF). A number that represents the present value of $1.00 discounted at an interest rate of *i* percent for *n* periods. A *present value interest factors table* shows the present value of $1.00 for various interest rates and a number of periods. *Contrast with* **future value interest factor (FVIF).**

present value interest factor for an annuity (PVIFA). A number that represents the present value of a $1.00 annuity at a given rate of interest and for a stated number of periods. *Contrast with* **future value interest factor for an annuity (FVIFA).**

present value of an annuity. The amount that must be invested now in order to provide for a specified, equally spaced series of equal future payments, given a specified interest rate and a specified number of periods. *Contrast with* **future value of an annuity.**

present value of an annuity due (PVAd). The amount that must be invested now in order to provide for a specified, equally spaced series of equal future payments made at the beginning of each payment period, given a specified interest rate and a specified number of periods. *Contrast with* **present value of an ordinary annuity (PVA).**

present value of an ordinary annuity (PVA). The amount that must be invested now in order to provide for a specified, equally spaced series of equal future payments made at the end of each payment period, given a specified interest rate and a specified number of periods. *Contrast with* **present value of an annuity due (PVAd).**

presumptive death certificate. A court-issued document stating that a person is presumed to be dead.

presumptive disability. According to the terms of some disability income policies, a stated condition that if present, automatically causes the insured to be considered totally disabled and thus eligible to receive disability income benefits. Examples of presumptive disabilities include total and permanent blindness or loss of two limbs.

pre-tax contributions. Contributions to a tax-advantaged account made with money on which income taxes have not yet been paid.

pretext interview. An interview in which one person attempts to gain information from another person by refusing to identify himself or herself, pretending to be someone else, or misrepresenting the purpose of the interview. In the United States, the National Association of Insurance Commissioners (NAIC) Model Privacy Act prohibits insurers or insurance sales agents from conducting pretext interviews.

pricing risk. *See* **C-2 risk.**

prima facie premium rates. In the United States, the maximum premium rates that state insurance laws permit insurers to charge for specific types of consumer credit insurance.

primary beneficiary. The party designated to receive the proceeds of a life insurance policy following the death of the insured. Also known as *first beneficiary*. *See also* **contingent beneficiary.**

primary care physician (PCP). In a managed health care plan, a physician, usually a general or family practitioner, who serves as the insured's personal physician and contact with the managed care plan.

principal. (1) In an agency relationship, the party that authorizes another party, the agent, to act on the principal's behalf in contractual dealings with third parties. (2) In investments, a sum of money originally invested; the amount of money upon which interest is calculated. (3) For an annuity, the amount of money the purchaser pays as premiums. (4) An officer or manager of a National Association of Securities Dealers (NASD) member, who is involved in the day-to-day operation of the securities business, has qualified as a registered representative, and has passed additional examinations. *See also* **registered principal**.

prior approval requirement. In the United States, a type of policy form filing requirement imposed by the states on individual and group life insurance, health insurance, and annuity policy forms; stipulates that a policy form must be filed with, and approved by, the state insurance department before the form is used in the state.

privileged information. According to the National Association of Insurance Commissioners (NAIC) Model Privacy Act in the United States, information about an individual that relates to either an insurance claim or a civil or criminal legal proceeding.

pro forma financial statements. In accounting, financial statements that project or estimate a company's financial condition based on current information and assumptions about company goals and activities.

probability. A numerical likelihood that a particular outcome will occur.

probationary period. In group insurance, the length of time—typically, from one to six months—that a new group member must wait before becoming eligible to enroll in a group insurance plan, as specified in the group master contract.

proceeds. The amount of money that an insurance company is obligated to pay for the settlement of an insurance policy. Proceeds may be a death benefit or the policy's cash or accumulated value.

producer. *See* **agent**.

product actuary. An expert in the mathematics of insurance and finance who determines the financial design of a new insurance product.

product line. *See* **line of business**.

product mix. *See* **product portfolio.**

product portfolio. The total assortment of products offered by a company. Also known as *product mix.*

professional association. An association of individuals who share a common occupation, such as an association of medical doctors, attorneys, or engineers. A professional association generally is considered to be an eligible group for group insurance purposes.

professional development. The completion of professional or educational programs and/or participation in professional organizations that enhance an individual's ability to perform a job.

professional liability insurance. Insurance that covers individuals who provide professional services, such as physicians and lawyers, from losses they incur as a result of being held responsible for the losses of their clients.

profit. *See* **net income.**

profitability ratios. Financial ratios that measure a company's profitability by comparing the company's gain from operations to the resources employed or invested to earn the gain.

profit center. In a business organization, a department or other business segment to which both costs (expenses) and revenues can be traced.

profit margin ratio. For a life insurance or an annuity product, a profitability ratio determined by dividing the product's present value of profits by the present value of premiums over the product's lifetime.

profit sharing plan. A type of defined contribution retirement plan that is funded primarily by employer contributions payable from the employer's profits. Contributions to a qualified plan must be substantial and recurring and cannot unduly benefit highly paid employees. Because employer contributions are based on profits, the amount of such contributions may vary from year to year.

profit-volume analysis. *See* **cost-volume-profit (CVP) analysis.**

projection method. A method for modifying mortality tables so as to account for a projected improvement in future mortality. The procedure involves multiplying the tabular rates by a chosen percentage. *Contrast with* **setback method.**

prolonged disability. As defined by the Canada Pension Plan and Quebec Pension Plan, a disability that is expected to be of long, continued, and indefinite duration or which is likely to result in death.

proofs of loss provision. An individual health insurance policy provision that specifies the time within which claimants must provide the insurer with proof of a covered loss.

property. An asset that can be owned or possessed.

property insurance. Insurance that provides a benefit payable if a specified property belonging to the insured is damaged, destroyed, or lost as the result of the occurrence of a specified risk, such as fire, theft, accident, or other cause described in the policy.

proportional reinsurance. A type of reinsurance coverage for which the ceding company and the assuming company agree to share premiums and claims according to a specified amount or a specified percentage at the time the reinsurance agreement is made. *See also* **reinsurance**, **ceding company**, and **reinsurer**.

proposal for insurance. In group insurance, a document that details the specifications of the plan proposed by an insurer for a proposed group, and that allows a proposed policyholder to compare the costs and benefits of the plan to those offered by other insurers.

proprietary mortality table. A mortality table developed by a single insurance company, based largely on the mortality rates the company has experienced with its own customers. *Contrast with* **published mortality table**. *See also* **mortality table**.

prospect. A potential buyer of a product or service.

prospecting. The process of identifying, contacting, and qualifying potential customers.

prospective reserve valuation method. For insurance companies, a method of computing a value for a reserve liability by finding the present values of a contract's future cash flows—its future premiums and future benefit payments. *Contrast with* **retrospective reserve valuation method**.

prospectus. A communication, usually written, that offers a security for sale and that must contain most of the information included in the security issuer's registration statement.

prospectus supplement. A document explaining any material changes to a security's investment characteristics that may be provided in lieu of a prospectus if a security undergoes a material change between the publication of two annual prospectuses. Also known as *sticker.*

provision for future policy benefits. *See* **policy reserve.**

proximate cause. For an accidental death or accidental disability insurance claim, the event that directly caused the death or disability, or the event that led to an unbroken chain of events resulting in death or disability.

prudent person approach. In the United States, a regulatory requirement that establishes statutory guidelines insurers are to follow in making investment decisions; requires an insurer to act as a prudent person would in making decisions about which assets the insurer includes in its investment portfolio.

public mortality table. *See* **published mortality table.**

published mortality table. A mortality table that shows the mortality rates experienced by the insurance industry as a whole. Also known as *public mortality table. Contrast with* **proprietary mortality table.**

punitive damages. In a lawsuit, money awards that are intended to punish an individual or entity that has acted in a malicious, fraudulent, or oppressive manner toward the plaintiff, and thus to dissuade others from similar behavior in the future. *See also* **compensatory damages.**

PV. *See* **present value.**

PVA. *See* **present value of an ordinary annuity.**

PVAd. *See* **present value of an annuity due.**

PVIF. *See* **present value interest factor.**

PVIFA. *See* **present value interest factor for an annuity.**

QPP. *See* **Quebec Pension Plan.**

qualification period. *See* **elimination period.**

qualified annuity. An annuity that is purchased to either fund or distribute funds from a tax-qualified employee benefit retirement plan and that is exempt from current income taxation during the accumulation period.

qualified beneficiaries. For purposes of the Consolidated Omnibus Budget Reconciliation Act (COBRA) in the United States, specified individuals who have the right to continue their group health insurance coverage following a qualifying event without providing evidence of insurability. *See also* **Consolidated Omnibus Budget Reconciliation Act (COBRA).**

qualified LTC plan. In the United States, a long-term care (LTC) insurance policy that is eligible for favorable tax treatment under federal law because it provides all the features required by the Health Insurance Portability and Accountability Act (HIPAA).

qualified retirement plan. In the United States, an employer-sponsored retirement plan that satisfies complex legal require-ments to receive federal income tax benefits. Known as a *registered plan* in Canada.

qualifying events. For purposes of the Consolidated Omnibus Budget Reconciliation Act (COBRA) in the United States, specified events—including the death of a covered employee and termination of a covered employee's employment—that would otherwise result in the termination of an individual's group health insurance coverage but that entitle the individual to continue the group health insurance for a limited time. *See also* **Consolidated Omnibus Budget Reconciliation Act (COBRA).**

quality rating. In the insurance industry, an alphabetical grade or rating assigned to an insurer by an insurance rating agency to indicate the level of the insurance company's financial strength, its ability to pay its obligations to customers, or its ability to pay its obligations to creditors.

Quebec Civil Code. In Canada, a regulation that governs all life and health insurance contracts in Quebec and specifies what provisions must be included in insurance contracts.

Quebec Pension Plan (QPP). A provincial pension plan that provides Quebec contributors and their families with benefits that are comparable to those provided by the Canada Pension Plan. The QPP provides retirement benefits, disability income benefits and survivor benefits to wage earners who reside in Quebec and who have contributed money into the plan during their working years.

quick liquidity ratio. For insurers, the ratio of an insurer's liquid assets to its contractual reserves. *See also* **ratio.**

quick ratio. One way of determining a company's ability to liquidate debt immediately, this ratio is calculated by dividing a company's most liquid current assets by the company's current liabilities. Also known as *acid-test ratio.*

quota share. (1) A type of proportional reinsurance in which a reinsurer agrees to accept a certain percentage of each insurance risk, and a ceding company retains the remaining percentage, up to a maximum retention limit. *See also* **proportional reinsurance.** (2) The portion of risk assumed by each reinsurer in a reinsurance pool.

RAA. *See* **retained asset account.**

ratchet method. *See* **annual reset method.**

rated policy. An insurance policy that is classified as having a greater-than-average likelihood of loss, usually issued with special exclusions, a premium rate that is higher than the rate for a standard policy, a reduced face amount, or any combination of these.

rate of return. Investment earnings expressed as a percentage relative to the invested principal. *See also* **principal.**

rate transmittal. In group insurance, a document that is attached to a Request for Proposal that specifies the agent's proposed rates for each type of insurance coverage for each class of employees. *See also* **Request for Proposal.**

rating. During the underwriting process for insurance, the act of approving an application on a basis other than the basis for which the policy was applied for, including actions such as approving the application at a higher premium rate than applied for or with less coverage than applied for. The resulting policy is said to be a *rated policy.*

rating agency. In the insurance industry, an independent organization that evaluates the financial condition of insurers and provides information to potential customers of and investors in insurance companies.

rating downgrade. A reduction in an insurer's quality rating. A downgrade often leads to a run on assets. *Contrast with* **rating upgrade.** *See also* **quality rating.**

rating upgrade. An increase in an insurer's quality rating. A rating upgrade is viewed as a sign of increased financial strength. *Contrast with* **rating downgrade.** *See also* **quality rating.**

ratio. A comparison of two numeric values that results in a measurement expressed as a percentage or a fraction. *See also* **financial ratio.**

RBC ratio requirements. *See* **risk-based capital ratio requirements.**

readability requirements. Insurance laws that require insurers to reduce the amount of technical jargon and legal language included in insurance and annuity contracts.

real estate. Land or anything attached to the land. *Contrast with* **personal property.**

realization principle. An accounting concept which states that a company should recognize revenue when it is earned, regardless of when the company receives the actual payment, so long as a legal and reasonable expectation exists that the customer will remit payment in full.

reasonable and customary limits. A restriction insurers include in medical expense policies which specifies that the amount paid for a claim must conform to the amount most frequently charged for a medical procedure in a given geographical area.

rebating. An insurance sales practice in which an insurance agent offers a prospect an inducement, such as a cash payment, to purchase an insurance policy from that agent. The practice of rebating is prohibited in most states.

recapture. A process by which a ceding company takes back from a reinsurer some or all ceded business.

recapture provision. In a reinsurance arrangement, a contractual provision that permits the ceding company to end or modify the reinsurance arrangement by taking back from the reinsurer some or all ceded business.

receivable. A type of short-term asset representing an outside party's promise to pay cash to the holder of the asset.

receivables for agents' debit balances. A short-term asset based on agents' obligations to an insurer.

receivables purchase agreement. A contract through which short-term assets known as receivables are sold for cash.

receiver. In the United States, the insurance commissioner, or someone acting on the commissioner's behalf, who is responsible for formulating a plan to distribute an impaired insurer's assets and for making sure that the insurer's obligations to customers are fulfilled to the greatest extent possible. Also known as *conservator*.

receivership. In the United States, a legal condition under which a state insurance commissioner takes control of and administers a financially impaired insurer's assets and liabilities. Also known as *conservatorship*.

reciprocal method. In accounting, a cost allocation method that fully recognizes the services that service departments perform for each other.

reciprocity. A reinsurance arrangement in which certain insurers and reinsurers agree to cede business to each other and assume risk from each other.

recording method. A method of changing the beneficiary of a life insurance policy under which the change is effective when the policyowner notifies the insurer in writing of the change. *Contrast with* **endorsement method.**

recording of transactions as executed. In accounting, when a company records all authorized and executed transactions in the correct accounting period, in the correct accounts, and in the correct monetary amounts.

recurring disability. In disability income insurance policies, a type of disability that is the result of the same cause as for an original disability and that reappears after the original period of disability and an intervening period of recovery.

redlining. A prohibited practice in which an insurer refuses coverage to an applicant, or cancels an insured's existing coverage, solely because of the applicant's or insured's geographic location.

reduced paid-up insurance option. One of several nonforfeiture options included in life insurance policies that allows the owner of a policy with cash values to discontinue premium payments and to use the policy's net cash value to purchase paid-up insurance of the same plan as the original policy. *See also* **nonforfeiture options**.

reduction provision. An insurance policy provision that reduces the amount of the benefit payable for a specified loss. *See also* **limitation**.

reexamination. In the United States, a regulatory examination of an insurance company that is conducted as a follow-up to a comprehensive or target examination and that is designed to determine whether the insurer has complied with recommendations or directives contained in a previous examination report.

referred lead. In sales, the name of a prospect that a client has given to a sales person or agent.

refinance. An action taken by borrowers when they repay their debt before repayment is due in order to make new borrowing arrangements at lower interest rates.

refund annuity. *See* **life income with refund annuity**.

refund life income option. A method of receiving life insurance policy proceeds under which the insurer uses the policy proceeds to purchase a life income with refund annuity for the beneficiary/payee. *See also* **life income with refund annuity** and **settlement options**.

regional office. An insurance company office that is charged with many of the same functions and operations as the company's home office but that is geographically closer to the market it serves and generally reports to the home office. *See also* **home office**.

registered plan. In Canada, a private retirement plan that meets the legal requirements to receive favorable federal income tax treatment. *See also* **qualified retirement plan**.

registered principal. An officer or manager of a National Association of Securities Dealers (NASD) member, who is involved in the day-to-day operation of the securities business, has qualified as a registered representative, and has an NASD Series 24 or 26 registration.

registered representative. A sales representative or other person who has registered with the National Association of Securities Dealers (NASD), disclosed the required background information, and passed one or more NASD examination. A registered representative engages in the securities business on behalf of a NASD member by soliciting the sale of securities or training securities salespeople.

registered retirement savings plan (RRSP). A Canadian retirement account that is similar to individual retirement accounts in the United States and that allows individuals or their spouses (not employers) to make tax-deductible contributions, subject to specified maximum amounts, for the purpose of accumulating money for retirement.

registration statement. A written statement containing detailed information about a security and the issuer of that security, including specified financial statements.

regular ordinary (RO) life insurance. Ordinary life insurance products sold through the home service insurance distribution system.

Regulation 60. A New York state insurance regulation designed to protect consumers against replacements that are not in the consumers' best interests. *See also* **replacement.**

regulations. Rules or orders that are issued by administrative agencies and that have the force of law.

regulatory compliance. *See* **compliance.**

Regulatory Information Retrieval System (RIRS). A database maintained by the National Association of Insurance Commissioners (NAIC) that contains information on insurance companies and individuals who have been the subjects of regulatory or disciplinary actions.

rehabilitation. (1) In disability income insurance, the process of helping a disabled person return to work, either at her own occupation or at another occupation if she is unable to perform the duties of her own occupation (2) In insurer insolvencies in the United States, a court-ordered process intended to restore a financially troubled company to a financially sound basis—the financially impaired insurer continues to operate and to exist. *Contrast with* **liquidation.** *See also* **receivership.**

reimbursement benefits. *See* **indemnity benefits.**

reinstatement. The process by which an insurer puts back into force an insurance policy that has either been terminated for nonpayment of premiums or continued as extended term or reduced paid-up coverage.

reinstatement provision. A provision in an individual life insurance, health insurance, or annuity policy that describes the conditions a policyowner must meet for the insurer to reinstate such a policy. *See also* **reinstatement.**

reinsurance. A transaction between two insurance companies in which one company—the *ceding company*—transfers some of its insurance risk to another company—the *reinsurer*. The reinsurer agrees to reimburse the ceding company for covered losses claimed under the policies that have been reinsured according to the terms of the reinsurance agreement. *See also* **ceding company** and **reinsurer.**

reinsurance allowance. In a reinsurance agreement, the payment from a reinsurer to a ceding company that represents a share of the ceding insurer's acquisition expenses and maintenance expenses for items such as commissions, underwriting costs, policy issue costs, and premium taxes.

reinsurance audit. A formal examination of an insurer's reinsurance records to evaluate whether those records contain accurate details and that ensures that both parties to a reinsurance agreement understand and have complied with the terms of the agreement.

reinsurance broker. *See* **reinsurance intermediary.**

reinsurance certificate. In a reinsurance arrangement, the document that notifies the ceding company that reinsurance is officially in force.

reinsurance company. *See* **reinsurer.**

reinsurance effective date. The date upon which the reinsurance coverage for a specific risk takes effect.

reinsurance intermediary. A third party that acts as a go-between for a ceding company and a reinsurer in effecting a reinsurance transaction. A reinsurance intermediary helps ceding companies find appropriate coverage for large-amount and unusual cases and can arrange for sufficient reinsurance from multiple reinsurers if no single reinsurance company will accept the entire risk. Also known as *reinsurance broker*.

reinsurance pool. In a reinsurance arrangement, a group of two or more reinsurers who accept risk from a given insurer.

reinsurance premiums. In indemnity reinsurance, premiums paid by a ceding company to a reinsurer for reinsurance coverage.

reinsurance recoverable. A type of account receivable that is recorded in an account titled *amounts recoverable from reinsurers.* This receivable represents a balance that a reinsurer owes to the insurer, usually for health insurance or another indemnity line of business.

reinsurance treaty. A formal written agreement that is negotiated and signed by a ceding company and a reinsurer and that establishes the terms and conditions by which risk can be submitted for reinsurance.

reinsurer. An insurance company that, for an exchange of value, such as a payment, accepts insurance risks transferred from another company—the *ceding company*—in a reinsurance transaction. Also known as *assuming company. See also* **ceding company.**

release. A written document that a recipient of life insurance policy proceeds must sign prior to receiving the policy's proceeds which states that the claimant has received full payment of his claim and that he gives up any and all claims that he has or might have against the insurer as a result of that policy.

relevance. In accounting, the quality of accounting information that requires a company's accounting information to be useful, timely, and likely to affect an interested user's decisions.

reliability. In accounting, the quality of accounting information that requires a company's accounting records and financial statements to present accurate, objective information that is free from bias and misrepresentation.

renewable term insurance policy. A term life insurance policy that gives the policyowner the option to continue the coverage at the end of the specified term without presenting evidence of insurability, although typically at a higher premium based on the insured's attained age.

renewal commission. A sales commission paid to an insurance sales agent for a specified number of years after the first policy year on policies that the agent sold. The renewal commission rate is generally lower than the first-year commission rate.

renewal expenses. *See* **maintenance expenses.**

renewal premium. Any insurance policy premium payable after the initial premium.

renewal provision. (1) A term life insurance policy provision that gives the policyowner the right, within specified limits, to continue the coverage for an additional policy term without providing evidence of insurability. (2) An individual health insurance policy provision that describes the circumstances under which the insurer has the right to refuse to renew or the right to cancel the coverage and the insurer's right to increase the policy's premium rate.

renewal underwriting. For group insurance plans, a type of underwriting in which the underwriter reviews all the risk assessment factors considered when the group was originally underwritten and all changes in the group and its coverage between the previous underwriting and the current time.

replacement. In insurance, a transaction that occurs when a policyowner surrenders an insurance policy or part of the coverage of a policy in order to buy another policy. Replacements may be external or internal. An *external replacement* occurs when the new policy is issued by a different insurer than the one that originally issued the policy. An *internal replacement* is one in which the new contract is purchased from the same insurer that issued the original contract.

replacement cost insurance. A type of homeowners' insurance that pays the policyowner the full cost of replacing the lost or damaged property, subject to a maximum amount.

Replacement of Life Insurance and Annuities Model Regulation. In the United States, a National Association of Insurance Commissioners (NAIC) model regulation that applies to life insurance policies and annuities that are being replaced and that is designed to ensure that insurers and agents provide consumers with fair and accurate information about policies so consumers can make buying decisions that are in their own best interests. *See also* **replacement.**

replacement ratio. In disability income insurance, the percentage of the insured's income that a disability policy will replace.

representation. A statement made by a contracting party that is relevant to the formation of the contract. Representations that are not substantially true will invalidate the contract. *Contrast with* **warranty.**

Request for Proposal (RFP). In group insurance, a document that provides detailed information about the requested coverage and requests a bid from the insurer for providing that coverage.

required capital. An insurance company's amount of capital and surplus to support financial obligations that arise from an insurer's existing book of business. Required capital allows the insurer to remain in business. Also known as *committed capital.*

required minimum distributions (RMDs). Amounts that participants in qualified retirement plans and owners of traditional individual retirement arrangements (IRAs) must begin to receive by a specified age or time. Also known as *minimum required distributions (MRD).*

required reserve. *See* policy reserve.

rescission. A legal action in which a contract is declared void or cancelled. An insurer usually seeks a rescission of an insurance policy when there has been a material misrepresentation in the insurance application. *See also* misrepresentation.

reserve. *See* reserves.

reserve credit. An accounting entry used by a ceding company to record the reduction of reserves, due to the use of reinsurance, in its Annual Statement or Annual Return. *See also* ceding company, reinsurance, and reinsurer.

reserve destrengthening. For an insurance company, the act of decreasing a reserve liability amount, which results in an increase in the insurer's capital or surplus. *Contrast with* reserve strengthening.

reserves. For an insurer, liability accounts that identify the amounts of money that the insurer expects to need to meet future business obligations. Although many different types of reserves exist, insurers use the term to refer to policy reserves. *See also* contingency reserve and policy reserve.

reserve strengthening. For an insurance company, the act of increasing a reserve liability amount, which results in a decrease in the insurer's capital or surplus. *Contrast with* reserve destrengthening.

reserve valuation. A formal actuarial process of establishing a value for an insurer's required policy reserves.

resident corporation. In Canada, a company that is incorporated under Canadian law. *See also* foreign corporation.

residual disability. In disability income insurance, a condition in which the insured is not totally disabled, but is still unable to function as before the sickness or injury, and therefore suffers a reduction in income of at least the percentage—typically 20 percent to 25 percent—specified in the disability income plan. Also known as *partial disability.*

residual disability insurance. *See* **income protection insurance.**

resisted claims. Claims that an insurer has thus far refused to pay but that it may pay in the future. Also known as *disputed claims.*

respite care. In long-term care (LTC) insurance, temporary care provided by a nursing home or other qualified LTC facility for an insured receiving home health care. Respite care is designed to give the primary caregiver in the home a break from the day-to-day care of the insured.

responsibility accounting. A system of policies and procedures that allows for revenues and expenses to be assigned to a specified employee or organizational level that is accountable for them.

responsibility center. The area, function, or organizational unit that a specified manager controls.

responsibility report. A management accounting report that itemizes budgeted and actual amounts that are under the responsibility manager's sphere of control and the corresponding variance for each revenue or cost (expense).

restoration of benefits provision. A provision in a long-term care (LTC) insurance policy that allows an insured person who has used a portion of benefits available under the LTC policy to regain a full benefit period after a stated period of time has passed following the delivery of the long-term care.

retained earnings. The profits that a corporation holds to reinvest in the business instead of paying the money out in dividends to the corporation's owners.

retention. *See* **persistency.**

retention limit. A specified maximum amount of insurance that an insurer is willing to carry at its own risk without transferring some of the risk to a reinsurer.

retired stock. Stock that a company had previously issued, then later repurchased at market price, with no intention of reselling the stock at a later date. *See also* **stock.**

retrocession. (1) A transaction by which a reinsurer cedes risks to another reinsurer, known as the *retrocessionaire.* (2) The unit of insurance that a reinsurance company cedes to a retrocessionaire.

(3) The document used to record the transfer of risk from a reinsurer to a retrocessionaire. *See also* **reinsurer, reinsurance,** and **retrocessionaire.**

retrocessionaire. A reinsurer that assumes risks transferred from another reinsurer. *See also* **reinsurer, reinsurance,** and **retrocession.**

retrospective rating arrangement. In group health insurance, a premium payment arrangement under which the insurer agrees to charge the group policyholder a lower monthly premium than it would normally charge based on the group's prior claim experience and the policyholder agrees to pay an additional amount if, at the end of the policy year, the group's claim experience has been unfavorable.

retrospective reserve valuation method. For insurance companies, a method of computing a value for a reserve liability by looking at a contract's past cash flows—its past premiums and benefits. *Contrast with* **prospective reserve valuation method.**

retrospective review. In a managed health care plan, the process in which the utilization review organization reviews the necessity and quality of the medical care an insured received in a hospital following the hospitalization. *See also* **managed health care plan** and **utilization review (UR).**

return. The profit or compensation an investor earns for taking a risk.

return of premiums option. In long-term care (LTC) insurance, a nonforfeiture option which provides that all or a portion of the premiums paid for the LTC coverage are returned to the policyholder.

return on investment (ROI). *See* **internal rate of return (IRR).**

Revenue Canada. *See* **Canada Customs and Revenue Agency.**

revenues. The amounts earned from a company's core business operations.

revocable beneficiary. A life insurance policy beneficiary whose right to the policy's proceeds can be cancelled or reduced by the policyowner at any time before the insured's death. *Contrast with* **irrevocable beneficiary.**

RFP. *See* **Request for Proposal.**

rider. An amendment or addition to a contract that either expands or limits the benefits payable under the contract. Also known as *endorsement. See also* **policy rider.**

RIRS. *See* **Regulatory Information Retrieval System.**

risk. The chance or possibility of loss.

risk assessment. In insurance underwriting, a process that involves ascertaining the degree of risk represented by each proposed insured person or group according to a range of criteria established when a specific insurance product was designed. Also known as *risk selection* and *selection of risks. See also* **underwriting.**

risk-based capital (RBC) ratio requirement. In the United States, requirements that enable state regulators to evaluate the adequacy of an insurer's capital relative to the riskiness of the insurer's operations.

risk class. In insurance underwriting, a grouping of insureds that represent a similar level of risk to an insurance company. *See also* **declined risk class, preferred risk class, standard risk class,** and **substandard risk class.**

risk-return tradeoff. An investment principle stating that the interplay between investment risk and return usually results in higher risks offering potentially higher returns, and lower risks offering potentially lower returns.

risk selection. *See* **risk assessment.**

risk tolerance. The degree to which a person is willing to accept financial risk.

RMDs. *See* **required minimum distributions.**

RO life insurance. *See* **regular ordinary life insurance.**

rolling budget. A budget that allows a company to continually maintain projections for a specified time period into the future. Also known as *continuous budget.*

rollover. A direct transfer of retirement funds from one qualified plan to another plan of the same type or to an individual retirement arrangement (IRA) that does not pass through the hands of the owner and thus does not incur any tax liability for the owner. Also known as *direct rollover* and *direct transfer.*

Roth IRA. In the United States, a type of individual retirement arrangement (IRA) that permits people within certain income limits to make nondeductible annual contributions and to withdraw money on a tax-free basis at retirement age.

routine checkup. In insurance underwriting, a visit to a physician that was not motivated by a symptom or health problem.

RRSP. *See* **registered retirement savings plan.**

Rules Governing Advertisements of Accident and Sickness Insurance. In the United States, National Association of Insurance Commissioners (NAIC) model regulation designed to prevent unfair, deceptive, and misleading advertising and ensure that insurers truthfully disclose the benefits provided by health insurance policies as well as any limitations and exclusions in those policies.

Rules Governing the Advertising of Life Insurance. In the United States, National Association of Insurance Commissioners (NAIC) model regulation designed to ensure that life insurance advertising materials provide full and truthful disclosure of all relevant information about a life insurance policy.

run on assets. A situation in which many customers at once demand to withdraw their funds from a financial institution.

S&L. *See* **savings and loan association.**

SAD. *See* **Special Activities Database.**

salaried sales distribution system. An agency-building insurance distribution system that relies on the use of an insurer's salaried sales representatives to sell and service all types of insurance and annuity products. *See also* **agency-building distribution system** and **salaried sales representative.**

salaried sales representatives. In the insurance industry, an insurance company salesperson who is a company employee and is paid a salary rather than commissions.

salary continuation plan. A short-term disability income insurance plan that provides 100 percent of an insured's salary, beginning on the first day of the insured's absence from work due to sickness or injury and continuing for some specified time.

sale-and-leaseback transaction. A method of financing using real estate, in which the owner of a building sells the real estate to an investor but immediately leases back the real estate from the investor.

sales agent. *See* **insurance agent.**

sales illustration. Promotional material used during or after a sales presentation to help explain complex products. Insurers often use graphic representations that show how an insurance policy's premiums, values, and benefits develop and change over a period of years. Also known as *policy illustration.*

sales presentation. The promotional message a sales person delivers to a prospect to explain, stimulate interest in, and motivate the prospect to purchase the product or products recommended in the proposal.

sales promotion. A company-sponsored program that is designed to motivate new sales activity and to offer one or several incentives for sales production.

sales revenue. The total dollar volume of sales.

sales volume. The number of units of product sold.

salvage value. The residual value or selling price of an asset at the end of its useful life.

SAP. *See* **statutory accounting practices.**

savings and loan association (S&L). A depository institution that gets the majority of its deposits from consumers and makes the majority of its loans as home mortgage loans. Also known as *savings bank* and *thrift.*

savings bank life insurance (SBLI). In the United States, life insurance coverage sold by authorized savings banks to people who live or work in the state in which the insurance is sold.

Savings Incentive Match Plan for Employees (SIMPLE). In the United States, a qualified retirement plan that may be established by small employers with 100 or fewer employees. (1) According to the terms of a SIMPLE individual retirement account (IRA), both the employer and employee can make tax-deductible contributions, up to a specified maximum, to an IRA that the employer has established for the employee. All earnings accumulate on a tax-deferred basis. (2) According to the terms of a SIMPLE 401(k) plan, both the employer and the employee can make contributions to the 401(k) plan up to a specified maximum. Employer contributions to the plan are deductible from the employer's current taxable income, employee contributions are on a pre-tax basis, and all earned income accumulates on a tax-deferred basis.

SBLI. *See* **savings bank life insurance.**

scenario analysis. A quantitative modeling technique that involves entering different sets of data into a model and then determining how changes in the input data affect the model's output.

scheduled net debt. For purposes of determining the benefit payable under a consumer credit insurance policy, the lump-sum amount needed to pay off the debt on a given date according to the credit agreement's repayment schedule.

schedule of benefits. (1) Under a group insurance plan, a table that specifies the amount of coverage provided for each class of insureds. (2) For medical expense claim purposes, a listing of medical treatments and the maximum benefit amounts an insurer will pay for each treatment.

schedules. In reinsurance arrangements, the provisions of the reinsurance treaty that cover the more variable elements such as the plans covered, retention limits, binding limits, and premium rates and allowances. Also known as *exhibits* and *conditions.*

seasoning requirement. In the United States, a licensing requirement that many states impose on foreign and alien insurers, which are eligible to receive a certificate of authority only if they have been actively engaged in the business of insurance for a specified time—usually three years. *See also* **alien corporation, certificate of authority,** and **foreign corporation.**

SEC. *See* **Securities and Exchange Commission.**

secondary beneficiary. *See* **contingent beneficiary.**

second excess. In a layering reinsurance arrangement involving two or more reinsurers, a specified amount of the remaining coverage above the first excess and up to a second, higher limit, that is ceded by the insurer to a second assuming company (or to a second group of assuming companies). *See also* **first excess** and **layering.**

second insured rider. A life insurance policy rider that provides term insurance coverage on the life of an individual other than the policy's insured. Also known as *optional insured rider* and *additional insured rider.*

Section 1035 exchange. In the United States, a tax-free replacement of an insurance policy for another insurance contract covering the same person that is performed in accordance with the conditions of Section 1035 of the Internal Revenue Code.

Section 7702. In the United States, a section of the Internal Revenue Code that defines the conditions a life insurance policy must satisfy to qualify as a life insurance contract.

secured bond. A bond in which the issuer pledges something of value to guarantee the safety of the bondholder's investment.

Securities Act of 1933. A U.S. federal law enacted to ensure that investors receive full and accurate disclosure of all information needed to make intelligent decisions when purchasing securities. Also known as *Truth in Securities Act.*

Securities and Exchange Commission (SEC). In the United States, the federal agency that has oversight authority over the securities industry, including the governance of the sale of securities.

securities broker. An individual, corporation, or other legal entity that is engaged in the business of buying and selling securities for the accounts of others.

securities exchange. A market in which buyers and sellers of securities (or their agents or brokers) meet in one location to conduct trades.

securities law. The body of law that governs the purchase and sale of securities.

security. A certificate that represents either ownership interest in a business (for example, a share of stock) or an obligation of indebtedness owed by an institution (for example, a bond). Also known as *financial instrument.*

segregated account. In Canada, an investment account that insurers maintain separately from a general account to help manage the funds placed in variable insurance products such as variable annuities. *See also* **separate account.**

segregated funds. *See* **segregated account.**

selection against the insurer. *See* **antiselection.**

selection of risks. *See* **risk assessment.**

select mortality table. A mortality table that shows the expected mortality rates of people who have recently been underwritten for insurance policies. *Contrast with* **basic mortality table** and **ultimate mortality table.**

self-administered group plan. A group insurance plan for which the group policyholder is responsible for handling the administrative and record-keeping aspects of the plan. *Contrast with* **insurer-administered group plan.**

self administration. A method of reinsurance administration in which the ceding company maintains detailed records for each ceded policy and provides the reinsurer with periodic reports outlining the risk ceded and premiums due.

self-insured group plan. A group insurance plan in which the group sponsor, not an insurance company, is financially responsible for paying the claims of the group insureds. A group may be partially or fully self-insured. Also known as *self-funded group insurance plan. Contrast with* **fully-insured group plan.**

SEP plan. *See* **simplified employee pension plan.**

separate account. In the United States, an investment account maintained separately from an insurer's general account to help manage the funds placed in variable insurance products such as variable annuities. *Contrast with* **general account.** *See also* **segregated account.**

separate account contract. A retirement plan funding vehicle under which plan assets are invested in an insurance company's separate accounts. A separate account contract usually does not guarantee investment performance. Also known as *investment facility contract.*

service fee. (1) Compensation paid to an insurance sales agent equal to a small percentage of the premiums payable after the renewal commissions have ceased. Also known as *persistency fee.* (2) In unbundled insurance products, a fee insurers charge customers that is generally deducted from the amount of the transaction being handled.

service requirement. In a group insurance plan, a required length of time—usually three to six months—that a person must be employed before being eligible for coverage under the group insurance plan.

setback method. A procedure for modifying mortality tables so as to account for the projected improvement in future mortality. The procedure involves using, for a specified age, a tabular mortality rate for a younger age or an older age. *Contrast with* **projection method.**

settlement options. Choices given to the owner or beneficiary of a life insurance policy regarding the method by which the insurer will pay the policy's proceeds when the policyowner does not receive the benefits in one single payment. Typically, the owner can elect (1) to leave the proceeds with the insurer and earn a specified interest rate, (2) to have the proceeds paid in a series of installments for a pre-selected period, (3) to have the proceeds paid in a pre-selected sum in a series of installments for as long as the proceeds last, or (4) to have the insurer tie payment of the proceeds to the life expectancy of a named individual through a life annuity. Also known as *optional modes of settlement. See also* **life annuity.**

settlement options provision. A life insurance and deferred annuity contract provision that grants the contract owner or beneficiary several choices as to how the insurer will distribute a contract's proceeds. Also known in annuity contracts as *payout options provision. See also* **payout options provision.**

sex-distinct mortality table. A mortality table showing different mortality rates for males and females at each age. Also known as *gender-based mortality table. Contrast with* **unisex mortality table.**

shareholder. *See* **stockholder.**

Sherman Anti-Trust Act. United States federal legislation that prohibits business dealings tending to create a monopoly.

Shopper's Guide to Long-Term Care Insurance. In the United States, a National Association of Insurance Commissioners (NAIC) publication designed to provide consumers with information about the long-term care insurance coverages that are available and to help consumers make informed purchase decisions.

short-term assets. Assets that a company expects to readily convert into cash or consume within the current accounting period, typically one year. *Contrast with* **long-term assets.**

short-term budget. A budget that generally covers a period of one year or less and relates mainly to a company's operations during that period. *Contrast with* **long term budget.**

short-term disability income insurance. A type of disability income coverage that provides disability income benefits for a maximum benefit period of from one to five years. *Contrast with* **long-term disability income insurance.**

short-term liabilities. In accounting, financial obligations that must be paid in one year or less. *Contrast with* **long-term liabilities.**

significant break in coverage. In the United States, and for purposes of the Health Insurance Portability and Accountability Act (HIPAA), a break of 63 days or more in an individual's creditable coverage.

SIMPLE. See **Savings Incentive Match Plan for Employees.**

simple interest. The type of interest that is earned on the original principal only. *Contrast with* **compound interest.**

simplified employee pension (SEP) plan. In the United States, a qualified employer-sponsored pension plan whereby an employer establishes and makes contributions into an individual retirement account or individual retirement annuity for each participating employee; however, the employee owns the account. Self-employed people also may establish a SEP plan.

single premium policies. A type of life insurance or annuity contract that is purchased by the payment of one lump sum. (1) A *single-premium deferred annuity (SPDA)* is an annuity contract purchased with a single premium payment whose periodic income payments generally do not begin until several years in the future. (2) A *single premium immediate annuity (SPIA) contract* is an annuity contract that is purchased with a single premium payment and that will begin making periodic income payments one annuity period after the contract's issue date. *Contrast with* **level premium policies** and **modified premium policies.**

six and six test. A requirement included in long-term care (LTC) insurance policies that states that an insured's long-term care is not covered if (1) the insured was treated for a condition within six months prior to the effective date of coverage and (2) the condition becomes the cause of long-term care within six months after the effective date of coverage.

small employer. For purposes of the Health Insurance Portability and Accountability Act (HIPAA) in the United States, an employer that has 50 or fewer employees.

small insurance company tax status. For purposes related to federal tax filings, a U.S. life insurance company with less than $15 million in taxable income and less than $500 million in assets.

social insurance supplement coverage. Insurance that provides benefits for medical expenses not covered by government programs.

Social Security. In the United States, a federal program that provides specified benefits, including a monthly retirement income benefit to people who have contributed to the plan during their income-earning years. The program also provides a benefit to qualified disabled individuals, as well as to the widows, widowers, and surviving dependent children of qualified deceased workers.

Social Security Disability Income (SSDI). A U.S. government program that provides monthly income benefits to qualified disabled individuals who are under age 65 and who have paid a specified amount of Social Security tax for a prescribed number of periods.

Society of Actuaries. An international organization that administers a series of actuarial examinations.

sole proprietorship insurance. A type of business insurance coverage that provides coverage on the life of the sole proprietor of a business—and can be used to pay the salary of hiring someone to run the business if the sole proprietor dies—or provides funds for a trusted employee or other person to buy a business at the death of the owner.

solvency. (1) A company's ability to meet its financial obligations on time. (2) For an insurer, the ability to maintain capital and surplus above the minimum standard of capital and surplus required by law. Also known as *statutory solvency*. In Canada, known as *capital adequacy*.

solvency-basis accounting records. *See* **statutory accounting records.**

solvency laws. Insurance laws that are designed to ensure that insurance companies are financially able to meet their debts and pay policy benefits when they come due.

solvency-profitability tradeoff. A relationship between solvency and profitability that can be summarized in the following manner: as the level of profitability increases, the risk of insolvency generally increases; as the level of profitability decreases, the risk of insolvency generally decreases.

source documents. The various business papers and electronic forms that contain original information about a company's financial transactions.

source of funds. *See* **cash flow.**

SPDA. *See* **single premium policies.**

Special Activities Database (SAD) In the United States, a database maintained by the National Association of Insurance Commissioners (NAIC) that enables state insurance regulators to exchange information about insurance companies and individuals who have been the subject of an insurance department investigation, have been charged with violations, or are suspected of engaging in unlawful activities.

special class rates. *See* **substandard premium rates.**

specialized medical questionnaire. An underwriting document that requests an attending physician to provide a proposed insured's detailed information on a specific illness or condition.

special risk. *See* **substandard risk class.**

special surplus. A part of a U.S. insurer's surplus that the insurer's board of directors has set aside to meet unforeseen contingencies or pay for certain extraordinary expenses. Also known as *appropriated surplus* and *contingency reserve*.

specified disease coverage. A type of health insurance coverage that provides benefits for the diagnosis and treatment of a specifically named disease or diseases, such as cancer. Also known as *dread disease coverage*. *Contrast with* **critical illness (CI) insurance.**

speculation. In insurance, the activity of purchasing insurance with the expectation of making a profit on the proceeds.

SPIA. *See* **single premium policies.**

split-dollar life insurance plan. An agreement under which a business provides individual life insurance policies for certain employees, who share in paying the cost of the policies.

split elimination period. For a health insurance policy, an increased waiting period for any claims related to an existing impairment, while the usual waiting period is applied to other claims.

split-funded plan. *See* **combination pension plan.**

spouse and children's insurance rider. *See* **family benefit coverage.**

spread. *See* **interest margin.**

spread-loss reinsurance. A type of nonproportional reinsurance in which benefits usually begin after the ceding company has paid 100 percent of the expected total annual claim amount as calculated by the ceding company's actuaries. *See also* **reinsurance.**

SSDI. *See* **Social Security Disability Income.**

staff model HMO. A type of closed panel health maintenance organization (HMO) in which the physicians who provide medical services for HMO members are employees of the HMO and generally operate out of offices in the HMO's facilities. *See also* **health maintenance organization (HMO)** and **closed panel HMO.**

standard premium rates. For insurance purposes, the premium rates charged insureds who are classified as standard risks.

standard risk class. In insurance underwriting, the group of proposed insureds who represent average risk within the context of the insurer's underwriting practices and therefore pay average premiums in relation to others of similar insurability. *Contrast with* **declined risk class, preferred risk class,** and **substandard risk class.**

Standard Valuation Law. In the United States, a National Association of Insurance Commissioners (NAIC) model law that establishes minimum requirements for calculating or valuing reserves for life insurance and annuity policies.

standby assistance. In long-term care (LTC) insurance, assistance that is in the form of observing or being close by an insured performing activities of daily living. *See also* **substantial assistance.**

state bank. In the United States, a bank that operates under a charter granted by a state regulatory agency and is subject to regulation and supervision by state regulators.

state insurance code. The portion of a state's legal code that is devoted to regulating the insurance industry.

state insurance department. In the United States, a state administrative agency that is charged with assuring that insurance companies operating within a state comply with all of that state's insurance laws and regulations.

statement of cash flows. A financial statement that provides information about the company's cash receipts, cash disbursements, and net change in cash during a specified period.

statement of operations. *See* income statement.

Statement of Policy Information for Applicant. A document that defines terms appearing in a universal life insurance policy contract and explains that many of the illustrated policy values are not guaranteed and, in some cases, are dependent upon the performance of equity-based investments. In the United States, the National Association of Insurance Commissioners (NAIC) Universal Life Insurance Model Regulation requires agents to provide this statement to consumers who apply for a universal life insurance policy.

statement of surplus. A financial statement that provides information about the change in an insurance company's surplus account during a specified period.

state of domicile. The state in which a company incorporates and has its principal legal residence. Also known as *domiciliary state.*

static budget. A budget that contains amounts that are generally not subject to change unless management has approved the changes.

static mortality table. A type of mortality table in which the rates have not been adjusted.

statistical phase of IRIS. The first phase of the Insurance Regulatory Information System (IRIS) used in the United States to monitor the financial condition of insurers. IRIS was established and is operated by the National Association of Insurance Commissioners (NAIC). In this phase, which is conducted annually, a system of financial ratio analysis is applied to the Annual Statement data of all insurers. During this analysis, an IRIS standard for each of twelve required financial ratios is compared with a company's actual financial ratios. Any unusual results require an analytical analysis of the company. *See also* **analytical phase of IRIS** and **Insurance Regulatory Information System (IRIS).**

statutory accounting practices (SAP). The accounting standards and methods that all insurers in the United States must follow when preparing the Annual Statement and specified other financial reports that are submitted to regulators. Also known as *statutory accounting principles.*

statutory accounting principles. *See* **statutory accounting practices (SAP).**

statutory accounting records. In the United States, accounting records designed for financial reporting to state insurance regulators, whose primary interest is in evaluating insurance companies' solvency and long-term financial stability. *Contrast with* **GAAP accounting records.**

statutory law. The type of law created by a legislative branch of government.

statutory minimum capitalization requirements. *See* **minimum capital and surplus requirements.**

statutory reserve. *See* **policy reserve.**

sticker. *See* **prospectus supplement.**

stock. A type of equity financial security that represents a share of ownership in a company. *See also* **common stock** and **preferred stock.**

stock bonus plan. A type of employee benefit savings plan that is funded primarily by employer contributions and that provides benefits in the form of shares of company stock.

stockbroker. *See* **broker-dealer.**

stock dividend. *See* **dividend.**

stock exchange. An organized marketplace where specific types of securities, such as common stock and bonds, are bought and sold by members of the exchange.

stockholder. A person or organization who owns stock in a company and, thus, partially owns that company. Also known as *shareholder.*

stockholder dividends. *See* **dividends.**

stock insurance company. An insurance company that is owned by the people who purchase shares of the company's stock. *Contrast with* **mutual insurance company.**

stock redemption insurance. *See* **stock repurchase insurance.**

stock repurchase insurance. A type of business insurance coverage that provides the remaining stockholders of a company with money to buy the stock of a deceased partner. Also known as *stock redemption insurance.*

stock subaccount. One of the three main asset classes in an insurance company's separate account within which owners of variable insurance contracts can deposit funds and have the funds invested in a variety of domestic and foreign stocks. *See also* **bond subaccount** and **money market subaccount.**

stop-loss insurance. Insurance purchased by employers that self-insure group health insurance plans so that they can place a maximum dollar limit on their liability for paying claims.

stop-loss provision. A health insurance policy provision which specifies that the policy will cover 100 percent of the insured's eligible medical expenses after he has incurred a specified amount of out-of-pocket expenses in deductible and coinsurance payments.

stop-loss reinsurance. A type of nonproportional reinsurance providing benefits for all claims that exceed a specified percentage of the total loss incurred above a certain amount during a specified period and/or a maximum dollar amount.

straight life annuity. A type of life annuity contract that provides periodic income payments for as long as the annuitant lives but provides no benefit payments after the annuitant's death. *See also* **life annuity.**

straight life insurance policy. *See* **continuous premium whole life insurance policy.**

structured settlement annuity. An immediate annuity issued to a person who is entitled to receive a specified sum of money from a third party; the terms of the annuity contract are structured to carry out the terms of the agreement between the annuitant and the third party.

subaccount. One of several alternative pools of investments within an insurer's separate or segregated account into which a variable contract owner may allocate premiums paid. Also known as *variable investment account* and *variable subaccount.* See also **general account, separate account,** and **segregated account.**

subrogation. (1) The legal right given to a creditor to be substituted for another and to succeed to the other's rights. (2) A legal right that permits an insurer to recover payments made to an insured when the insured received payment for the claim through a separate legal action.

subsidiary. A company that is owned and controlled by another company, but that operates separately from the controlling company.

substandard premium rates. The premium rates charged insureds who are classified as substandard risks. Also known as *special class rates.*

substandard risk class. In insurance underwriting, the group of proposed insureds who represent a significantly greater-than-average likelihood of loss within the context of the insurer's underwriting practices. Also known as *special class risk. Contrast with* **declined risk class, preferred risk class,** and **standard risk class.**

substantial assistance. For purposes of the Health Insurance Portability and Accountability Act (HIPAA) in the United States, the type of assistance that a person insured under a long-term care policy must need in order to qualify for payment of policy benefits. The Internal Revenue Service has defined substantial assistance to include both standby assistance and hands-on assistance. *See also* **hands-on assistance** and **standby assistance.**

succession beneficiary clause. *See* **preference beneficiary clause.**

successor beneficiary. *See* **contingent beneficiary.**

successor payee. *See* **contingent payee.**

suicide exclusion provision. A life insurance policy provision stating that policy proceeds will not be paid if the insured dies as the result of suicide as defined within the policy within a specified period following the date of policy issue.

summary plan description. For employee benefit plans, a written document that is understandable by the average plan participant and that reasonably informs participants and beneficiaries about their rights and obligations under the plan. In the United States, the Employee Retirement Income Security Act (ERISA) requires employers that sponsor employee benefit plans to provide employees with a summary plan description.

Superintendent of Insurance. The director of a provincial Office of the Superintendent of Insurance. *See also* **Office of the Superintendent of Insurance.**

Superintendents' Guidelines. A series of recommendations to insurers adopted by the Canadian Council of Insurance Regulators in cooperation with the Canadian Life and Health Insurance Association (CLHIA).

supplemental coverage. An amount of coverage that adds to the amount of coverage specified in a basic insurance policy.

supplementary notice. In the United States, a notice that the Fair Credit Reporting Act (FCRA) requires underwriters who use consumer and investigative consumer reports to provide insurance applicants with in certain circumstances; this type of notice must be sent within five days of a consumer's request for information regarding the nature and scope of the investigation specified in the pre-notice.

surplus. For an insurer, an amount that represents the assets a company has over and above its reserves and other financial obligations.

surplus note. A special type of unsecured debt security, issued only by insurance companies, that has characteristics of both traditional equity securities and traditional debt securities.

surplus ratios. *See* **capital and surplus ratios.**

surplus relief. An arrangement to diminish potential surplus strain. The amount of the surplus relief. *Contrast with* **surplus strain.**

surplus relief ratio. An insurer's net cost for or net earnings from ceding and assuming reinsurance to the insurer's capital and surplus. A type of financial leverage ratio. *See also* **ratio** and **surplus relief.**

surplus strain. A decrease in an insurer's surplus, amounting to a financial loss caused by the high initial costs and the reserve requirements associated with new products. Also known as *new business strain. Contrast with* **surplus relief.**

surrender. *See* **cash surrender value.**

surrender charge. (1) An amount charged to an annuity contract owner when he prematurely withdraws a portion or all of the contract's accumulated value. Also known as *back load, contingent deferred sales load,* and *withdrawal charge.* (2) Expense charges imposed on some types of life insurance policies when the policyowner surrenders the policy.

surrender cost comparison index. A cost comparison index, used to compare insurance policies, which takes into account the time value of money and measures the cost of a policy over a 10- or 20-year period assuming the policyowner surrenders the policy for its cash value at the end of the period. *Contrast with* **net payment cost comparison index.**

surrender value. *See* **cash surrender value.**

survivor benefits. Periodic income benefits paid to specified dependents of an insured or an annuitant who survive the death of the insured or the annuitant.

survivorship clause. *See* **common disaster clause.**

suspense account. In accounting, a temporary account where deposited funds can be held until the billing statement has been processed and the funds have been allocated to the appropriate accounts.

SWP. *See* **systematic withdrawal program.**

systematic and rational allocation. An accounting concept which states that a company expenses an asset's cost over its estimated useful life, regardless of when the company receives revenues from the asset.

systematic withdrawal program (SWP). An arrangement by which a deferred annuity contract owner makes withdrawals at regular intervals from the annuity's accumulated value.

table of underwriting requirements. For each insurance product, a document that specifies the kinds of information the underwriter must consider in assessing the insurability of a person who is proposed for coverage under that policy.

table rating method. In determining premium charges for life insurance, an approach to charging for substandard risks by dividing those risks into broad groups according to their numerical ratings.

tabular mortality. *See* **expected mortality.**

tabular mortality rate. A mortality rate shown in a mortality table.

tangible asset. In accounting, an asset that has physical form. *Contrast with* **intangible asset.**

target market. A group of consumers to whom a business will attempt to sell a particular product.

target market conduct examination. In the United States, an examination by state insurance regulators of one or more specific areas of an insurer's operations to ensure that those operations are in accordance with state insurance laws and regulations. *Contrast with* **comprehensive market conduct examination.** *See also* **market conduct examination.**

tax cost basis. The amount of money contributed to an annuity that will not be subject to taxation because it has already been taxed.

tax-deferred basis. Accumulation of investment income on which income taxes are not payable until money is withdrawn from the investment vehicle.

tax-qualified employee benefit plan. An employee benefit plan, such as a retirement plan, that is eligible to receive favorable federal income tax treatment.

Tax Sheltered Annuity (TSA). In the United States, a retirement annuity sold only to organizations offering qualified retirement plans under section 403(b) of the U.S. Internal Revenue Code. *See also* **403(b) plan.**

tax withholding. A deduction for income taxes that is taken from a disbursement and sent to a federal, state, or provincial tax authority and that reduces the amount of income taxes that must later be submitted.

T-bills. *See* **treasury bills.**

team underwriting. A method used to organize underwriting work in which underwriters are divided into small groups, usually including one or more senior underwriters who handle large-amount or complex cases, and one or more lower-level underwriters who handle simpler cases.

technical design. For an insurance product, the phase of product development that involves creating the product language, product provisions, pricing and dividend structures, and underwriting and issue specifications.

telemarketing. A direct response sales method that uses the telephone to produce sales.

Telephone Transfer Authorization. Permission given by a life insurance or annuity contract owner authorizing the insurer to act on subaccount transfer requests communicated over the phone.

teleunderwriting. An underwriting method by which a home office employee or a third party administrator, rather than the sales agent, takes responsibility for gathering much of the information needed for underwriting.

temporary account. In accounting, an account that is zeroed out to a permanent account on the balance sheet at the end of each accounting period.

temporary flat extra premium method. In life insurance, an approach to charging for substandard risks that involves adding an amount to the premium for an impairment for which the extra mortality risk is expected to decrease and eventually disappear over a limited time period.

temporary insurance agreement (TIA). A premium receipt given by an insurer to an insurance applicant, at the time an insurance policy is applied for and when the initial premium is paid, that provides insurance coverage of a specified amount for a specified time, usually for the time required to underwrite the case. Also known as *binding premium receipt.*

ten-day free look provision. *See* **free-look provision.**

terminal illness (TI) benefit. *See* **accelerated death benefit.**

term life insurance. Life insurance that provides a death benefit only if the insured dies during the period specified in the policy. If the insured survives until the end of the period, coverage ceases without value. *Contrast with* **permanent life insurance.**

term to maturity. For investments, the amount of time that must pass before an asset can be converted to cash for an approximation of its value.

third-party administrator (TPA). (1) An organization that provides administrative services for customers of a financial services company. (2) In group insurance, an organization that administers group benefit plans for a self-insured group but that does not have financial responsibility for paying benefits.

third-party applicant. In life insurance, a person who applies for coverage on the life of another person.

third-party distribution system. *See* **nonagency-building distribution system.**

third-party notification provision. A provision in a long-term care (LTC) insurance policy that allows the policyowner to designate a person for the insurer to contact in the event that the policyowner misses a premium payment.

thrift and savings plan. In the United States, a retirement savings plan to which an employer is obligated to make contributions on behalf of an employee if the employee makes a specified contribution to the plan.

thrifts. *See* **savings and loan (S&L) association.**

TIA. *See* **temporary insurance agreement.**

time clause. *See* **common disaster clause.**

time limit on certain defenses provision. An individual health insurance policy provision that limits the time during which the insurer may contest the validity of the contract on the ground of misrepresentation in the application or may reduce or deny a claim on the ground it results from a preexisting condition. *See also* **incontestability provision.**

time of payment of claims provision. An individual health insurance policy provision which states that after receiving written proof of loss for which the policy provides periodic benefit payments, the insurer will pay those benefits as described in the policy.

time-period concept. An accounting principle stating that a company's financial statements should report the company's business operations during a specified time period, usually referred to as an accounting period.

top-down budgeting. A budgeting process that begins with a company's senior management and is passed down to lower-level management.

top-heavy plan. A retirement plan under which, for a given plan year, the present value of accrued benefits for key employees exceeds a specified percentage of the present value of accrued benefits for all employees.

total asset turnover. A financial ratio that measures how efficiently a company has used its total assets to generate revenues.

total disability. For disability insurance purposes, an insured's disability that meets the requirements of the definition of total disability included in the disability insurance policy or policy rider and that qualifies for payment of the specified disability benefits. When a disability begins, total disability is usually the complete and continuous inability of an insured to perform the essential duties of his regular occupation. After a disability has existed for a specified period, total disability usually exists only if the insured is prevented from working at any occupation for which he is reasonably fitted by education, training, or experience. *See also* **disability** and **residual disability**.

total leverage. A combined effect of operating leverage and financial leverage—represents the effect whereby incurring fixed costs automatically magnifies both risks and potential returns to a company's owners. *See also* **positive leverage effect**.

TPA. *See* **third party administrator**.

trade association. An association of firms that operate in a specific industry.

trail commissions. *See* **asset-based commissions**.

transaction confirmation. For annuity contracts, a document that an insurer sends to the contract owner showing the details of an annuity transaction. For variable annuities, the Securities and Exchange Commission (SEC) requires insurers to send a confirmation of each financial transaction that is not a regularly scheduled transaction. Also known as *confirmation statement*.

transaction processing system. An organized collection of procedures, software, databases, and devices used to record high-volume, routine, and repetitive business transactions.

transfer fee. For variable annuities, an amount an insurer charges for the administrative processing of an asset transfer between subaccounts. A transfer fee usually is charged once a customer's number of transfers within a given period has exceeded the contract's maximum.

transfer for value rule. In the United States, a federal income tax rule stating that when the ownership of a life insurance policy has been transferred for a valuable consideration, policy proceeds paid following the insured's death are taxable to the recipient to the extent the proceeds exceed the total amount the recipient paid for the policy.

transfer price. In accounting, the price of a good or service that one business segment or line of business charges another segment or line of the same company.

transplant donor benefit. A disability income policy benefit that specifies that if an insured undergoes surgery to donate a part of his body to another person, the insurer will treat that surgery as a sickness and will pay benefits for it.

treasury bills (T-bills). A type of low risk security issued and guaranteed by the U.S. government that can easily be converted into cash.

treasury stock. Stock that has been repurchased at market price by the issuing company with the intention of reselling the stock at a later date.

trend. A change that occurs over time.

trend analysis. A type of financial analysis that involves calculating percentage changes in financial statement items over several successive accounting periods, rather than over just two periods.

trust. A legal arrangement whereby one or more persons—called the *trustees*—hold legal title to property on behalf of another person—called the *trust beneficiary*—and are responsible for administering the property for the benefit of the trust beneficiary.

trust beneficiary. *See* **trust.**

trustee. *See* **trust.**

trusteed pension plan. A type of pension plan that is funded through a trust arrangement. The plan sponsor chooses a trustee, usually a bank or a trust company, that invests the contributions and pays benefits in accordance with the trust agreement. Also known as *uninsured plan* and *self-administered plan*. *Contrast with* **combination pension plan** and **fully-insured pension plan.**

Truth in Lending Act. In the United States, a federal consumer protection law that requires creditors that deal with consumers to make certain written disclosures concerning finance charges and related aspects of consumer credit transactions and that establishes requirements for the advertising of credit terms.

TSA. *See* **Tax Sheltered Annuity.**

turnaround time. For the customer service function, the amount of time necessary to complete a particular customer-initiated transaction.

twisting. An illegal insurance sales practice, in which a sales agent misrepresents the features of a contract in order to induce the contract owner to replace his current contract, often to the disadvantage of the contract owner. *See also* **misrepresentation.**

tying. A prohibited insurance sales practice in which a financial institution makes the completion of one financial transaction, such as approval for a loan, dependent upon another financial transaction, such as the purchase of insurance.

UCR fee. *See* **usual, customary, and reasonable fee.**

UL. *See* **universal life insurance.**

ultimate mortality table. A mortality table that shows the expected mortality rates of people who have not recently been underwritten for insurance policies. *Contrast with* **basic mortality table** and **select mortality table.**

umbrella liability insurance. Insurance that provides additional liability coverage over and above that provided by a homeowners', automobile, professional liability, or comprehensive personal liability policy.

unallocated pension funding contract. A type of pension plan contract in which some or all of the plan sponsor's contributions are held in a pooled account and are not attributed to plan participants until the time arrives for the disbursement of benefits. *Contrast with* **allocated pension funding contract.**

unassigned surplus. *See* **divisible surplus.**

unauthorized insurer. In the United States, an insurer that does business in a particular state without becoming licensed to do business in that state in accordance with that state's law. Also known as *nonadmitted insurer.*

unauthorized reinsurer. A reinsurance company that is not licensed, admitted, accredited, authorized, or otherwise recognized by the insurance department in the jurisdiction of a ceding company.

unbundled product structure. Insurance or annuity product design in which an insurer explicitly discloses various expense charges to customers and also specifies the rate of investment return being credited to customers. *Contrast with* **bundled product structure.**

uncollected premiums. For U.S. insurers, individual life insurance premiums and annuity considerations that were due on or before the Annual Statement date, but for which the insurer has not received payment by that date. These amounts are called premiums outstanding in Canada. *See also* **premiums outstanding.**

undeliverable. Term used for an insurance policy that is refused by the buyer when the agent attempts to deliver it. Also referred to as *not taken.*

underinsured motorists coverage. Insurance that protects an insured and his passengers when the other driver has insurance coverage, but that coverage is inadequate to cover their injuries. *See also* **uninsured motorists coverage.**

underwriter. The person in an insurance company who evaluates proposed risks, accepts or declines insurance applications, and determines the appropriate premium amount to charge acceptable risks.

underwriting function. The area within an insurance company that is responsible for (1) assessing and classifying the degree of risk represented by a proposed insured or proposed group with respect to a specific insurance product and (2) making a decision concerning the acceptance of that risk.

underwriting guidelines. An insurer's general standards that specify the parameters within which a proposed insured may be assigned to a risk class for a particular insurance product.

underwriting manual. A paper or electronic guide to underwriting action that includes the information an insurer uses to assign relative values to life insurance risks and typically provides descriptive information on impairments.

underwriting objective. *See* **underwriting philosophy.**

underwriting philosophy. A set of objectives for guiding all of an insurer's underwriting actions that generally reflects the insurer's strategic business goals and includes its pricing assumptions for products. Also known as *underwriting objectives.*

underwriting worksheet. For a particular insurance case, a document that contains records of telephone calls and other communications, documentation of requests for reinsurance, underwriting requirements and other information requested, and other notations that explain clearly the manner in which the case has been handled from the time it was submitted to the insurer.

undirected deposit. For an annuity contract, a contribution for which the contract owner gives no specific instructions as to how the deposit should be allocated among the available subaccounts.

unearned income. The subset of collected income that has been collected but not yet earned.

unearned premium. A portion of the insurance premium received in one period, but applicable to the insurance coverage to be provided in the following period but before the next policy anniversary date.

Unemployment Insurance Act. In Canada, federal legislation that provides covered individuals with protection against loss of income resulting from unemployment. Benefits are provided for covered employees who are laid off or who are unable to work due to accidental injury, sickness, or pregnancy.

Unfair Claims Settlement Practices Act. In the United States, a National Association of Insurance Commissioners (NAIC) model act that specifies a number of actions that are unfair claim practices if committed by an insurer transacting business in the state in conscious disregard of the law or so frequently as to indicate a general business practice.

Unfair Trade Practices Act. A law that many states have enacted that defines certain business acts as unfair and prohibits those practices in the business of insurance.

unfavorable variance. In accounting, a cost variance in which the actual cost is higher than the standard cost. Also known as *unfavorable deviation. Contrast with* **favorable variance.**

Uniform Accident and Sickness Insurance Act. A model law adopted by the Canadian Council of Insurance Regulators (CCIR) and enacted by all of the common law provinces of Canada to regulate health insurance contracts.

Uniform Individual Accident and Sickness Policy Provision Law (UPPL). In the United States, a National Association of Insurance Commissioners (NAIC) model law that specifies the provisions individual health insurance policies must contain.

Uniform Life Insurance Act. Model legislation governing life insurance contracts agreed upon by the Canadian of Council of Insurance Regulators (CCIR) and enacted with minor variations by all of the common law jurisdictions of Canada.

unilateral contract. A contract between two parties, only one of whom makes legally enforceable promises when entering into the contract. *See also* **bilateral contract.**

uninsurable risk class. *See* **declined risk class.**

uninsured motorists insurance. Insurance that covers an insured driver and her passengers for physical injuries incurred in an accident with a driver who carries no liability insurance. *See also* **underinsured motorists insurance.**

uninsured plan. *See* **trusteed pension plan.**

unisex mortality table. A mortality table that shows a single set of mortality rates that reflect one mortality rate for both males and females at each age. *Contrast with* **sex-distinct mortality table.**

unit cost. (1) The incurred expense attributable to a single measured amount of work. (2) In insurance, the amount charged per $1,000 of coverage, based on the level of risk presented by a specific insured. Also known as *cost of insurance rate.*

unit of coverage. A basic amount of insurance coverage that insurers use when calculating premiums for their products. For life insurance, a unit of coverage usually is $1,000 of coverage.

universal life II. *See* **variable universal life insurance.**

universal life (UL) insurance. A form of permanent life insurance characterized by flexible premiums, flexible face amounts, and unbundled pricing factors.

unpaid premiums provision. An individual health insurance policy provision which states that when a claim is paid, any premium due and unpaid may be deducted from the claim payment.

unrealized gain (or loss). A gain (or loss) that has not become actual because the investment has not matured or been sold.

UPPL. *See* **Uniform Individual Accident and Sickness Policy Provision Law.**

UR. *See* **utilization review.**

usage variance. In accounting, the difference between the actual quantities to be sold or processed and the budgeted quantities sold or processed, multiplied by the budgeted rate.

use of funds. *See* **cash flow.**

usual, customary, and reasonable (UCR) fee. The maximum dollar amount of a given covered expense that the insurer will consider as eligible for reimbursement under a medical expense policy.

utilization review (UR). A process by which a managed health care plan evaluates the necessity and quality of an insured's medical care, using techniques such as preadmission certification, concurrent review, and retrospective review. *See also* **concurrent review, preadmission certification,** and **retrospective review.**

valid contract. A contract that is enforceable at law. *Contrast with* **void contract.** *See also* **voidable contract.**

validation period. The amount of time required for a product to become profitable or for an insurance product to begin contributing to surplus. Also known as *break-even period.*

validation point. An insurance-specific version of a break-even point, it is the point at which a product's asset share is equal to the policy reserves for the product. *See also* **asset share** and **break-even point.**

valuation. (1) The formal process of calculating the monetary value of a company's assets, liabilities, and owners' equity. (2) The process of setting reported values for an insurer's invested assets. In the United States, insurers must comply with state laws that specify how to determine the value of invested assets for statutory reporting purposes.

valuation actuary. An expert in the mathematics of insurance who specializes in rendering a professional opinion as to proper values for an insurance company's assets and liabilities.

valuation mortality table. A type of mortality table used for calculating statutory reserves (solvency reserves) and that has a safety margin built into the mortality rates.

value-added activity. An activity that makes a product more valuable to the customer.

valued contract. A type of insurance contract that specifies in advance the amount of the benefit that will be payable when a covered loss occurs, regardless of the actual amount of the loss incurred. A life insurance policy is a valued contract. *Contrast with* **contract of indemnity.**

variable annuity. An annuity under which the amount of the accumulated value and the amount of the periodic annuity benefit payments fluctuate in accordance with the performance of a specified pool of investments. Premiums paid for a variable annuity are deposited into an insurer's separate account in the United States and segregated account in Canada. Within a separate or segregated account, the insurer maintains many subaccounts that allow the contract owner to invest in a wide variety of investments. The contract owner assumes most of the annuity contract's investment risk. *Contrast with* **fixed annuity.**

variable budget. *See* **flexible budget.**

variable contract. An insurance or an annuity contract in which the contract owner allocates the premiums paid among one or more pools of investments, known as *subaccounts*. A variable contract may offer a fixed-interest subaccount, but, under most of the subaccounts offered, the investment results are variable. Variable contracts offer only limited guarantees as to investment return, cash accumulation value, or death benefit.

variable cost. A business cost that changes in direct response to changes in the level of operating activity. *Contrast with* **fixed cost.**

variable interest rate. An interest rate that fluctuates according to the rise and fall of interest rates in the marketplace.

variable investment account. *See* **subaccount.**

variable life (VL) insurance. A form of permanent life insurance in which premiums are fixed, but death benefits and other values may vary, reflecting the performance of the subaccounts in an insurer's separate account.

Variable Life Insurance Model Regulation. In the United States, a National Association of Insurance Commissioners (NAIC) model law that establishes qualifications an insurer must meet in order to market variable life insurance and specifies requirements that variable life insurance policies must meet.

variable payout option. A variable annuity payout option whereby the insurer makes a series of annuity payments that vary throughout the payout period based on the performance of the underlying subaccounts.

variable-premium life insurance policy. *See* **indeterminate premium life insurance policy.**

variable subaccount. *See* **subaccount.**

variable universal life (VUL) insurance. A form of permanent life insurance that combines the premium and death benefit flexibility of universal life insurance with the investment flexibility and risk of variable life insurance. With this type of policy, the death benefit and the cash value fluctuate according to the contract's investment performance. Also known as *universal life II.*

vertical analysis. A type of financial analysis that reveals the relationship of each financial statement item to a specified financial statement item during the same reporting period. *Contrast with* **horizontal analysis.**

vested. The status of a retirement plan participant who has met requirements giving her the right to receive partial or full retirement benefits even if she terminates employment prior to retirement.

vested commission. In insurance sales, a commission that is guaranteed payable to an agent even if the agent no longer represents the company when the commission comes due.

viatical company. An organization that buys life insurance policies from people who have catastrophic or life-threatening conditions or illnesses.

vision care coverage. Supplemental medical expense coverage that provides benefits for expenses incurred in obtaining eye examinations and corrective lenses.

VL. *See* **variable life insurance.**

void contract. A contract that cannot be legally enforced by either party and that creates no legal obligation for either party to carry out the terms of the agreement. *Contrast with* **valid contract.** *See also* **voidable contract.**

voidable contract. A contract in which one party has the right to avoid his or her obligations under the contract without incurring legal liability to the other party. *See also* **valid contract, void contract,** and **voidable contract.**

VUL. *See* **variable universal life insurance.**

waiting period. For a health insurance policy, the period of time that must pass from the date of policy issue before benefits are payable to an insured. Also known as *elimination period* and *probationary period.*

waiver. The voluntary and intentional relinquishment of a known legal right.

waiver of premium for disability (WP) benefit. A supplementary life insurance policy or annuity contract benefit under which the insurer promises to give up its right to collect premiums that become due while the insured is disabled according to the policy or rider's definition of disability.

waiver of premium for payor benefit. A supplementary benefit provided by some juvenile insurance policies under which the insurer promises to give up its right to collect the policy's renewal premiums if the adult policyowner dies or becomes totally disabled prior to the insured child's attainment of a specified age, usually 21.

waiver of premium provision. In long-term care (LTC) insurance, a policy provision that allows an insured person to stop paying premiums at a specified point while the insured person is receiving long-term care and the policy is making benefit payments.

waiver of surrender charge provision. In an annuity contract, a provision specifying that the insurer will not impose a surrender charge on withdrawals under certain conditions, such as the unemployment or disability of the contract owner.

war exclusion provision. A life insurance policy provision that limits an insurer's liability to pay a death benefit if the life insured's death is connected with the war or military service as defined in the insurance policy.

warranty. A promise or guarantee that a statement of fact is true. The statement is made by a party to a contract at the time of contracting, becomes a part of the contract, and if not literally true, gives the other party a ground to rescind the contract. *Contrast with* **representation**.

welfare benefit plan. According to the Employee Retirement Income Security Act (ERISA) in the United States, any plan or program that an employer establishes to provide specified benefits, including life and health insurance benefits, to plan participants and their beneficiaries.

whole life insurance. A type of life insurance that remains in effect, if the premiums are current, until the insured dies. Whole life insurance builds a cash value for the policyowner. *Contrast with* **term life insurance**.

window premiums. Additional premiums paid on a single-premium deferred annuity during the first contract year.

withdrawal. For a deferred annuity, payment of a portion of the annuity's accumulated value to the contract owner during the accumulation period. Also known as *partial withdrawal* and *partial surrender*.

withdrawal charge. *See* **surrender charge**.

withdrawal provision. An annuity contract provision that permits an insured to reduce the amount of the contract's accumulated value by taking up to that amount in cash. Also known as *partial surrender provision*.

work division system. A system for organizing underwriting work that divides cases according to the person or group that underwrites them; examples include independent underwriting, team underwriting, jet unit underwriting, and committee underwriting.

workers' compensation. Government-mandated insurance that provides benefits to covered employees and their dependents if the employees suffer job-related injury, disease, or death.

Workers' compensation programs exist in both Canada and the United States.

worksite marketing. An insurance sales process that involves offering individual and/or group insurance products to employees in their workplace on a voluntary, payroll-deduction basis.

WP benefit. *See* **waiver of premium for disability benefit.**

yearly renewable term (YRT) insurance. One-year term life insurance that is renewable at the end of the policy term. Also known as *annually renewable term (ART) insurance. See also* **term life insurance.**

yearly renewable term (YRT) reinsurance method. A reinsurance premium payment method under which a ceding company pays a one-year term insurance premium to the reinsurer on the anniversary date of each reinsured policy.

zero-based budgeting (ZBB). A budgeting process in which a company begins with the premise that no resources will be allocated for the next accounting period unless and until each expense is shown to be in accord with the company's strategic and operational goals.